LIBERTY'S CHILDREN

Stories of Eleven Revolutionary War Children

SCOTTI COHN

Lauren,
I hope you enjoy meeting these children!

Scotti Cohn
11-13-04

TWODOT®

GUILFORD, CONNECTICUT
HELENA, MONTANA
AN IMPRINT OF THE GLOBE PEQUOT PRESS

A · TWODOT® · BOOK

Library of Congress Cataloging-in-Publication Data
Cohn, Scotti.
Liberty's children: stories of eleven Revolutionary War children / Scotti Cohn.—1st ed. p. cm.
Includes bibliographical references (p.) and index.
Contents: The greatest terror and confusion : John Greenwood—An actor in the scenes of war : Andrew Sherburne—No safety for you here: Mary Hunt Palmer—Worthy of praise : James Durham—A spirit warm and bold : Deborah Samson—Not born to be drowned : Ebenezer Fox—Troublesome times : James Potter Collins—So tired, so sad, and so scared : Frances Slocum—With liberty for all : James Forten—Prepare to hear amazing things : Sally Wister—Almost beyond endurance : Christopher Hawkins.
ISBN 0-7627-2734-9
1. United States—History—Revolution, 1775-1783—Participation, Juvenile. 2. United States—History—Revolution, 1775-1783—Children. 3. Children—United States—Biography. 4. Children—United States—History—18th century. I. Title

E209.C34 2004
973.3'083—dc22 2004051623

Manufactured in the United States of America
First Edition/First Printing

To Ray
for yesterday, today, and tomorrow

CONTENTS

ACKNOWLEDGMENTS

I wish to express my gratitude to the people who helped make this book possible. In particular, I thank Susan Westbury of Illinois State University's history department for her generous gifts of time and knowledge. I also thank editors Charlene Patterson, Erin Turner, and Amy Hrycay. Others who deserve mention are: the librarians and staff of Illinois State University; Paul Carnahan, Vermont Historical Society; William Copeley, New Hampshire Historical Society; Linda Davis, descendant of Ebenezer Fox; Linda Grant De Pauw, Professor Emeritus of History, The George Washington University; Tom Green, Texas Society, Sons of the American Revolution; Don N. Hagist, Brigade of the American Revolution; Jesse Lemisch, Professor Emeritus of History, John Jay College of Criminal Justice of the City University of New York; Kerry McLaughlin, The Historical Society of Pennsylvania; Dana Signe K. Munroe, Rhode Island Historical Society; Barbra Nadler, Sharon Public Library, Sharon, Massachusetts; Ellen Royce, descendant of James Potter Collins; Meryl Rutz, author of paper on Ebenezer Fox; Paul J. Schueler, Tippecanoe County Historical Association, Lafayette, Indiana; Timothy Shannon, Gettysburg College; and Michael K. Smith, Louisiana Genealogical Register.

INTRODUCTION

When Americans think about the American Revolution, certain names come quickly to mind—George Washington, Patrick Henry, Paul Revere, John Paul Jones, and Samuel Adams. These men deserve to be remembered, yet their stories cannot give us a clear picture of what life was like for the average person during the years before, during, and immediately after the war.

History books usually do not describe how a nine-year-old Massachusetts boy might have felt when his friend was killed in the Boston Massacre or what went through the mind of a teenage Quaker girl when her family fled Philadelphia. Although we learn that Native Americans were pressured to choose sides in the war, we may not hear how their involvement affected a five-year-old Pennsylvania girl. We typically do not read about the trials that would have been faced by a fourteen-year-old African-American boy captured at sea or what it was like for a tailor's apprentice from South Carolina to stand in the front lines at the Battle of the Cowpens.

These are the kinds of stories you will find in this book: stories of children and young people caught up in the currents of a war that lasted eight long years. Many of these children not only survived the war but also played an active role in it. They took up the challenge of carrying the new nation's ideals into the future.

THE GREATEST TERROR AND CONFUSION

John Greenwood

1760–1819

The Boston Gazette and Country Journal listed the names of the dead on March 12, 1770. Among them were Crispus Attucks, a runaway slave, and Samuel Maverick, "a promising youth of seventeen years of age . . . an apprentice to Mr. Greenwood."

"Tuesday morning presented a most shocking scene," the newspaper story read. "The blood of our fellow citizens running like water through King Street and the Merchants' Exchange, the principal spot of the military parade for about eighteen months past."

Whether soldiers or civilians were more to blame for the deadly incident was not clear. The indisputable fact was that on Monday night, March 5, eighteen people had been shot by British troops in Boston. Five died from their wounds.

The American newspaper called the event a "horrid massacre." To the British officer in charge, it was a "melancholy affair." For many, the Boston Massacre, as it came to be known, was a very personal tragedy. This was true for nine-year-old John Greenwood.

John's father was the "Mr. Greenwood" mentioned in the newspaper account of the Boston Massacre. He was an ivory turner and part-time dentist. Samuel Maverick, his apprentice, had lived with the Greenwoods while learning the ivory-turning trade, and John Greenwood and Samuel Maverick had shared a room.

Dealing with the sudden, violent death of a close friend and roommate was hard on such a young boy. Decades later he still remembered going to bed as soon as it was dark that night, hoping to see Samuel's spirit. "I was so fond of him and he of me," he wrote in his memoirs, "that I was sure [his ghost] would not hurt me. The people of New England at that time pretty generally believed in hobgoblins and spirits, that is the children at least did."

Samuel's ghost failed to appear, and John was left to mourn his friend in a less fanciful manner.

Born in Boston in 1760, John Greenwood was the son of Isaac and Mary I'ans Greenwood of Massachusetts. Until age thirteen, John attended the North Writing School in Boston. John described his education in his memoirs, warning readers not to demand too much of him. "As children were not at that time taught what is called grammar, or even correct spelling," he wrote, "it must not be expected to find them in this relation."

John claimed that everything the boys learned was "thumped in" by two masters who barely had time to do more than flog those who misbehaved. One of the men, John Tileston, was particularly harsh in dealing out punishment. Even after John Greenwood grew up and became a father, he still crossed to the other side of the street to avoid "the venerable Mr. Tileston."

While John was just eight or nine years old, he began to take part in an activity that was destined to bring him misfortune. The activity was not alcohol consumption—although the child often drank beer (it was readily available to people of all ages), nor did it involve behaving badly in school. Instead, what should have been a harmless pastime became, in John's words, "the sole cause of my travels and disasters."

"About this period," he wrote years later, "I commenced learning to play upon the fife."

Although the British military presence in Boston offended

many of the town's citizens, John loved the fife-and-drum music the soldiers played. One day he found an old fife, repaired a crack in the instrument with putty, and learned to play several tunes. Soon he was good enough to be a fifer in the local militia. In the military, the fife was used for much more than entertainment. Musicians used their instruments to signal their comrades, conveying orders from officers to the soldiers. The country was at peace then, and John had no way of knowing where his musical skills would lead him.

In 1773, at age thirteen, John was sent to live with an uncle in Falmouth, Massachusetts. By then the rumblings of war were being heard loudly and clearly throughout the colonies. Americans disguised as Indians dumped barrels of British Tea into Boston Harbor. Tarring and feathering became a favorite form of punishment for political opponents.

"The whole country at this time was in commotion," John recalled in his memoirs. "And nothing was talked of but war, liberty, or death . . . Every old drunken fellow they found who had been a soldier, or understood what is called the manual exercise, was employed of evenings to drill them."

John's uncle, who may or may not have been a "drunkard," was an officer in an independent military company. Before long the members of that company were marching in time to John's fife.

Two years passed, and in April 1775 John and his uncle heard disturbing news. "We had an account that the British troops had marched out of Boston, attacked the country people at a place called Lexington, and killed a number of them," John recalled later.

John was worried about his family in Boston, but his uncle would not give him permission to go to them. John was not so easily deterred. Without telling anyone, he set out on foot in early May.

"Sunday morning, when in New England all is still and no persons are in the streets, having eaten my breakfast, I took a handkerchief and tied up in it two or three shirts and a pair or two of stockings, and with what clothes I had on my back and four and a half pistareens in my pocket, jumped over the fence in the back yard and set off."

John could not have expected to get very far on the small amount of money he had. A "pistareen," or peseta, was a small silver coin worth about a quarter of a dollar. Luckily, the fifteen-year-old also had his fife. Fife music was in demand, especially among people preparing to march to Boston to fight the British.

"Stopping at the taverns where there was a muster," he wrote later, "I played them a tune or two. Thus by the help of my fife I lived, as it were, on what is usually called free-quarters nearly upon the entire route."

Among the songs popular at the time was "War Song," which included the lines:

> Hark, hark, the sound of war is heard,
> And we must all attend;
> Take up our arms and go with speed,
> Our country to defend.
>
> Then let us go against our foe,
> We'd better die than yield;
> We and our sons are all undone,
> If Britain wins the field.

John arrived at Charlestown in good shape. To his disappointment, he was stopped by a sentry who refused to let him continue across the river to Boston, which was under British control.

"There I stood alone," John wrote. "Without a friend or a house to shelter me for the night, surrounded by women and children, some crying and others in different situations of distress, for the Boston people were flocking out of town over the ferry in crowds."

John entered a tavern, where he encountered a few people he knew. They encouraged him to enlist in the army as a fifer, assuring him that the enlistment would be for only eight months, and that he would be paid. The men were confident the British would soon be driven from Boston, at which time John could rejoin his family.

This plan made sense to John, although he considered the American troops to be little more than "a mob" at that point. Soon he and his fellow patriots were quartered in an Episcopal minister's vacated house.

"There we stayed," he wrote. "To call it living is out of the question, for we had to sleep in our clothes upon the bare floor. . . . I remember well the stone which I had to lay my head upon."

After about three weeks, John obtained a furlough to visit his great-aunt, who lived 20 miles away. He set out briskly, but as he drew near to the town where she lived, a strange feeling came over him. "There was a certain something that prevented me from going forward; it seemed to push me back or, as it were, insist on my returning."

John tried to resist but could not. As soon as he turned back toward the camp, the feeling of uneasiness left him. The long walk tired him, however, and he had to stop for the night at a farmhouse, where he ate a meal of "mush and milk." Early on the morning of June 17, 1775, he was on his way again, a sense of urgency propelling him toward camp.

With the dawn came the sound of gunfire, and John learned that British and American troops were engaged in a deadly struggle. The Americans wanted to control Charlestown Peninsula, joined to the mainland by a narrow neck of land and separated from Boston by the Charles River. Originally, they planned to fortify Bunker Hill, the high point of the peninsula. However, Maj. Gen. Israel Putnam, a fifty-seven-year-old veteran of the French and Indian War, decided Breed's Hill was a better choice because it was closer to Boston. A few troops were left at Bunker Hill to cover any retreat. Putnam later became famous as the man who commanded "Don't fire until you see the whites of their eyes!"

As John passed through Cambridge common on that clear,

calm, summer day, he was shocked by what he saw. "Everywhere the greatest terror and confusion seemed to prevail," he recalled. "And as I ran along the road leading to Bunker Hill it was filled with chairs and wagons, bearing the wounded and dead, while groups of men were employed in assisting others, not badly injured, to walk. . . . I could feel my hair stand on end."

John wished he had never enlisted as a soldier. A man staggered by, bleeding from a wound in the back of his head. Horrified, John asked him if it hurt much. The man shrugged and said no. He told John he planned to get the wound treated and go back into battle. Suddenly, John felt less anxious than before. "I began to feel brave and like a soldier from that moment," he wrote. "And fear never troubled me afterward during the whole war."

For six hours, while the Americans were digging trenches along the high ground, the English bombarded them from the water. During the next two-and-a-half hours, 1,200 to 1,500 patriots fought against 2,500 British troops, land-based artillery, a 68-gun ship of the line, two floating artillery batteries, a frigate, an armed transport, a pair of gunboats, and two sloops of war.

John joined his regiment on the road in sight of the battle. His captain was surprised to see him and asked why he had returned so soon from his furlough. John replied that he had heard cannon fire early in the morning and considered it his duty to be with his fellow soldiers. "I thought I might as well appear brave as not," he explained in his memoirs, "and make myself to be thought so by others."

Indeed, as he reported later, his comrades regarded him as "a brave little fellow."

The British marched straight up Breed's Hill against the fortified American lines. The first few volleys the patriots fired felled nearly one hundred of the enemy. Stunned but not defeated, the British regrouped for a second attack. A third assault took them over the parapets and into the midst of the exhausted and grossly outnumbered defenders.

"At last the bayonet went to work," John wrote later. "And as the majority of the Americans, using fowling-pieces, had no weapons of this kind, and as many even had no more powder, they clubbed their guns and knocked the enemy down with the butt-ends. But at last, for the want of bayonets and powder, they were obliged themselves to retreat and leave the English in possession of a dear-bought little piece of ground."

During the battle the British had fired carcasses—hollow shells filled with combustibles—at Charlestown, which was now in flames.

"The fools!" John declared. "It was of no great advantage to them, as it made a great smoke which the wind blew directly on both combatants."

The British now held the ground all the way to Charlestown Neck. However, they had little cause for celebration. More than 800 of their troops had been wounded, and another 226 were dead. In contrast, only 140 Americans had been killed, 271 wounded. The odds against the patriot "mob" had been enormous, yet they had inflicted great damage on the elite forces of King George III.

"After the battle," John later wrote, "little else was done by either party except the building of breastworks and forts, as the enemy were by this time convinced that we would sell every inch of ground at as dear a rate as we could."

John's friends at the tavern had been wrong when they persuaded him to enlist. The British had not been driven from Boston, and he still could not reach his parents. In spite of its impressive showing, the patriot "army" was little more than a rabble. It did not have a unified command and was short on military supplies, money, and discipline.

Following their retreat from Breed's Hill, the patriots built camps and fortifications on Prospect Hill, in a district of Charlestown dominated by seven tall hills. In John's words, the main structure was "a common dirt fort made of ground and covered with sods of grass, mounting about eight or ten iron guns, from 9- to 18-pounders." British and American sentries in the area were so close to each other that, according to John, "conversation used to be carried on between those of either side."

In early July, Gen. George Washington arrived in Cambridge to take charge of 16,000 to 17,000 American troops. It was his responsibility to turn them into a real army. He faced significant challenges. Many of the soldiers had, like John Greenwood, enlisted only for the short term. Watching General Washington ride by, John never imagined that he would one day have a highly unusual connection to the man. For the time being, however, the war was the main focus of attention.

"Night was the time for frolicking," John wrote in his memoirs. "As the British were constantly sending bombs at us, and sometimes from two to six at a time could be seen in the air overhead, looking like moving stars in the heavens."

Unlike the Americans, the British seemed to have plenty of gunpowder to waste.

"Some of our sentries were placed in very dangerous situations, much-exposed to the fire of the enemy," John recalled. "We, however, became so accustomed to this that nothing was thought of it, and for half a pint of aniseed water one soldier who was a little timid could get another to stand for him as sentry in the most perilous place." The ever persuasive "aniseed water" was a strong, highly flavored liqueur made from wine and the seeds of the anise plant.

Throughout the fall and winter of 1775, the standoff around Boston continued. John's term of enlistment expired in December, and he reenlisted for another year. In March 1776, Washington's troops seized and fortified Dorchester Heights, which until then had not been occupied by either side. On the morning of March 17, the British pulled out of Boston. John provided this explanation in his memoirs: "When the British perceived that it would be impossible to drive us from Dorchester Heights without another Bunker Hill frolic, or one much worse, they concluded to quit the town, not burning it if we let them go quietly; so we permitted them to depart, with their braggadocios, in peace."

A few days later John's regiment marched to New York. In April his unit proceeded to Canada, where he served under Gen. Benedict Arnold. In Montreal nearly two-thirds of the regiment came down with smallpox, but John managed to avoid catching the frequently fatal disease.

The Canadian campaign was a disaster for the colonists, who were defeated by harsh weather and a British army that greatly outnumbered them. As the colonial troops retreated toward New York, John's regiment stopped in Montreal for a few days. Most of the men had smallpox and needed whatever rest they could get. The British soon caught up with the colonists and the alarm was sounded: "Retreat! Retreat! The British are upon us!"

"Down we scampered to the boats," John wrote. "Those of the sick who were not led from the hospital crawling after us. Camp equipage, kettles, and everything were abandoned in the utmost confusion. . . . When halfway across the river it began to grow very dark, and down came the rain in drops the size of large peas, wetting our smallpox fellows, huddled together like cord-wood in the boats, and causing the death of many."

Once on shore, John took refuge in an old barn, where he discovered other soldiers with the same idea. The men were "lying on the floor close together like hogs," he recalled. "So I contentedly pigged it down with the rest, not knowing who they were nor caring if they had been devils so long as I could have got a warm berth among them."

In spite of their losses, the patriots were able to prevent British forces from invading the lower 13 colonies from Canada at that time. However, the British did invade America from Canada less than a year later.

By November 1776 John was back in New York. He had remained healthy until this point, but he now suffered from "fever and ague." En route from Albany to Trenton, New Jersey, he and his comrades bore the brunt of Mother Nature's wrath.

"It rained, hailed, snowed, and froze," he later recalled, "and at the same time blew a perfect hurricane . . . I recollect very well that at one time, when we halted on the road, I sat down on the stump of a tree and was so benumbed with cold that I wanted to go to sleep; had I been passed unnoticed I should have frozen to death . . . but as good luck always attended me, Sergeant Madden came and, rousing me up, made me walk about."

In December John fought in the Battle of Trenton, which resulted in an American victory. His enlistment term ended and, weak from his illness, the sixteen-year-old collected his pay and went home. "I had then been in the army twenty months and had received during that time only six months' pay for all my services," he declared in his memoirs. "I have never asked nor applied to Congress for the residue since, and I never shall."

At age nineteen, John joined the crew of an American privateer—a privately owned ship commissioned by the government. He was captured and imprisoned in a dungeon in Barbados, West Indies. Conditions were horrendous, yet the men somehow managed to keep up their morale. Years later, John still remembered the words to a song he learned from an elderly prisoner. Family and friends often heard him singing:

> This world, my dear Myra, is full of deceit,
> And friendship's a jewel we seldom can meet;
> How strange does it seem when in looking around,
> That source of content is so scarce to be found.

After John was released, he recuperated at home for a time, then enlisted on another privateer. He was captured at least twice but escaped each time.

Following the war, John repaired watches, compasses, barometers, and mathematical instruments. He also tried his hand at wood turning, the art of shaping wood into forms on a lathe. In the 1780s, after receiving basic instruction from his father, John opened a dental practice in New York.

George Washington was plagued with bad teeth most of his adult life, and in 1789 the newly elected president became one of John's patients. John carved several sets of ivory dentures for President Washington. At least one set consisted of a cow's tooth, one of Washington's teeth, hippopotamus ivory, metal, and springs. Until his death in 1799, Washington continued to use John's services. In the years that followed, John advertised himself as "dentist to the late President George Washington."

By 1800 John was considered by many to be New York City's leading dentist. He invented the first known "dental foot engine" by adapting his mother's foot-treadle spinning wheel to rotate a drill.

John Greenwood died November 16, 1819, several months after suffering a stroke. He was fifty-nine years old. He was survived by his wife, Elizabeth Weaver Greenwood, and four children: Jane, Clark, John, and Isaac John. According to Greenwood family records, John was buried in "the family vault in the old Brick Church, corner of Beekman Street and Chatham (Park) Row." His remains were later moved and "are now at rest in Greenwood Cemetery."

AN ACTOR IN THE SCENES OF WAR

Andrew Sherburne

1765–1831

In 1765, to help defray the cost of maintaining British soldiers in the American colonies, the British Parliament passed the Quartering Act and the Stamp Act. The Quartering Act required the colonies to provide barracks and supplies for British troops. The Stamp Act taxed newspapers, legal documents, and other printed matter.

Many Americans felt these acts added insult to injury. The colonists did not want British soldiers in their midst in the first place, and they resented these efforts to collect money for the Crown. In response, John Adams of Massachusetts drafted a Stamp Act Protest. His second cousin, Samuel Adams, organized a secret society called the Sons of Liberty to oppose the act. Down in Virginia, Patrick Henry led members of the House of Burgesses in preparing a set of resolves that argued that only Virginia's governor and legislature had the right to tax Virginians. "If this be treason," Henry declared ominously, "make the most of it."

That same year on September 30, Andrew Sherburne was born in Rye, New Hampshire. His parents, Andrew and Susannah Knight Sherburne, already had two sons, Thomas and Samuel, and a daughter, Marthy. Gazing at their new baby in his cradle, they must have had many thoughts. Certainly they hoped little Andrew would be one of the lucky ones—a child who survived in spite of diseases such as diphtheria, scarlet fever, and smallpox, which were all too common in those days.

Andrew's parents also may have wondered what lay in store for their son if he did survive. When he was old enough, of course, he would be sent to live with a tradesman as an apprentice. His master would provide food and lodging for the boy while training him. Andrew might become a tanner, a shoemaker, a metalworker, or furniture builder.

Mr. and Mrs. Sherburne probably did not imagine that in less than a decade, America would be at war with England, fighting for independence. Looking at their tiny son as he slept, they could not possibly have foreseen the role he would play—while still very young—in the birth of a new nation.

In 1766 New Hampshire acquired a new royal governor: John Wentworth. He had not been in office even a year when Parliament passed the Townshend Acts, imposing duties on lead, glass, paint, tea, and paper imported into the colonies. The money was to be used for military expenses and to pay the salaries of the royal colonial officials. Not surprisingly, this act, along with several other provisions passed at the same time, pushed Americans closer to rebellion.

Amid the mutterings of discontent, Andrew Sherburne grew from infant to toddler. By the time he reached age four, the Stamp Act had been repealed. However, Americans were still protesting other taxes levied by Parliament. In an effort to control unrest, King George III had sent British troops to Boston.

New Hampshire shared a border with Massachusetts but so far had not experienced the upheaval seen in its neighbor to the south. Its economy prospered. The capital city of Portsmouth continued to thrive, beautified by Georgian mansions built during the twenty-four-year tenure of Benning Wentworth, the current governor's uncle. In 1769 Dartmouth College was opened in Hanover.

Soon enough, however, the time came when New Hampshire could no longer remain aloof from the increasing hostilities between Britain and America.

In March 1774 the British Parliament voted to close the port of Boston as punishment for an incident that would go down in history as the Boston Tea Party. The people of New Hampshire were not united in their reaction. In general the wealthier citizens tended to remain loyal to the Crown. Support for rebellion came mostly from the province's farmers, mechanics, artisans, tradesmen, lumbermen, and fishermen. Clergy from the Congregational church threw their influence behind the patriot cause as well. Congregationalists were by far the largest body of believers in the colony.

With British General Thomas Gage and his troops firmly in control of Boston, the people of New Hampshire were concerned that they might receive similar treatment. Their worst fears were realized on December 13, 1774, when Paul Revere rode into Portsmouth. Revere, a silversmith and ardent patriot from Boston, brought news that the British might be planning to take over Fort William and Mary in Portsmouth Harbor.

The next day a group of approximately 400 New Hampshire patriots attacked the fort, easily overpowering the six men assigned by Governor Wentworth to defend it. The patriots seized nearly one hundred barrels of gunpowder, which they redistributed among various provinces.

After denouncing the raid on Fort William and Mary, Governor Wentworth discovered that many individuals disagreed with him, and that some of those individuals had a violent nature. No longer willing to pretend he was running the colony, he fled for his life.

By the time shots were fired at Lexington and Concord, Massachusetts, in the spring of 1775, the men of New Hampshire had reached their boiling point. Almost 10,000 volunteers from that colony immediately headed for Boston. Although long on enthusiasm, they were short on organization and discipline. In addition, according to a citizen of New Ipswich, the men who gathered in his town wore homespun flax shirts, loose vests, oversized coats, close-fitting knee pants (called smallclothes), long stockings, and cowhide shoes adorned with large buckles. "Not a pair of boots graced the company," he noted. The lack of uniforms emphasized the fact that these men were not professional soldiers.

Andrew Sherburne, who had not yet turned ten, was living with his family in Londonderry, New Hampshire, about 45 miles northwest of Boston. He watched as the militiamen of Londonderry marched away. Like those in New Ipswich, they carried a variety of weapons—swords made from farming utensils and guns of every shape, size, and vintage, with a few with bayonets attached.

Trouble continued around Boston. In June a patriot attempt to hold Breed's Hill on the Charlestown Peninsula failed. Andrew heard about the defeat of the American troops and the subsequent burning of Charlestown. Many years later, at the age of sixty-two, he set pen to paper to describe what he remembered: "The young men went off to the battleground, prompted by their sires who followed them with their horses laden with provisions, and I wished myself old enough to take an active part."

Other boys felt the same way. "Lads from seven years old and upwards were formed into companies," Andrew wrote in his memoirs. "And being properly officered, armed with wooden guns, and adorned with plumes, they would go through the manual exercise with as much regularity as the men."

In March 1776, a statement called the Association Test was circulated in the American colonies for signature among all white males age twenty-one and older. By signing it, men promised "to oppose the Hostile Proceedings of the British Fleets and Armies against the United American colonies." The purpose of the document was to give the newly formed Congress an idea of how much support existed for independence.

By this time the Sherburnes were living in Portsmouth. Nearly

500 Portsmouth men signed the Association Test, among them Andrew Sherburne's father. About thirty men were either absent or refused to sign.

In Portsmouth the Revolution seemed much more real to Andrew than it had in Londonderry. "Ships were being built, prizes taken from the enemy unloaded, and privateers fitted out," he recalled. "Nearby, soldiers drilled, and the roar of cannon and the sound of martial music so infatuated me, I was once again filled with anxiety to become an actor in the scenes of war."

All Andrew could think about was the drama, the excitement, and the adventures that awaited anyone who signed up to fight. The prospect of serving aboard a sailing ship particularly appealed to him because his older brother Thomas had just returned from a cruise.

Still a few months shy of his fourteenth birthday, Andrew considered himself almost a man. He hinted to his sister that if his parents did not allow him to go to sea, he would run away. Many boys his age and younger were doing exactly that.

Andrew was so obsessed with the subject he even talked about it in his sleep. His mother overheard him and told his father. The Sherburnes decided it would be better to help their son choose a ship than to forbid him to go. That way they would at least know where he was.

"My father . . . preferred the service of Congress to privateering," Andrew wrote later. "My two half-uncles, Timothy and James Weymouth, were on the *Ranger*."

The Weymouths assured Mr. Sherburne that they would look out for his son. Before long, Andrew found himself assigned to the boatswain, an officer responsible for the work of the other seamen. Andrew's job was to run errands and, if the ship was in a battle, to carry cartridges.

Andrew was new to life at sea, but his ship, the *Ranger*, was not. Built in Portsmouth early in 1777 for the Continental navy, it had been reconfigured by John Paul Jones, a native of Scotland.

Jones used the sloop to raid the Irish coast. He captained the *Ranger* for two years, then took command of the *Bonhomme Richard*. Not long after that, upon being asked to surrender to the captain of Britain's HMS *Serapis*, Jones uttered his now-famous declaration: "I have not yet begun to fight."

By the time Andrew joined the crew of the *Ranger*, Thomas Simpson was its captain. "Being ready for sea, we sailed to Boston and joined the *Providence*, the *Boston*, and the *Queen of France*," Andrew recalled. "I believe that this small squadron composed nearly the entire navy of the United States."

He was not too far off. At the beginning of 1779, the Continental navy consisted of only about a dozen ships. Fortunately, Congress had commissioned privately owned ships and individual states had their own navies as well. The *Ranger* headed out to sea in June, with Andrew aboard. He quickly became acquainted with one of the more unpleasant aspects of traveling by ship. "The sea was rough," he later wrote. "Many were exceedingly sick, myself among the rest, and we afforded a subject of constant ridicule to the old sailors."

Another of Andrew's concerns with life on the "bounding main" had to do with language. "My aversion to swearing had rendered me an object of ridicule," he recalled. "I had been insulted and frequently obliged to fight . . . I was sometimes victorious. Nevertheless, I finally decided to indulge in swearing." His swearing "caused some remorse." He counteracted that by being "more constant in praying."

The *Ranger* returned home in August, having participated in the capture of about ten ships loaded with sugar, cotton, ginger, allspice, and rum. Andrew was pleased to rejoin his family. In his absence, his mother had given birth to another daughter, bringing the count of Andrew's siblings to three brothers and seven sisters.

In a few weeks Andrew was ready for another cruise on the *Ranger*. This time, after taking "a few small British transports of little value," the *Ranger* encountered "four or five large British ships of war" off the coast of Florida. The enemy gave chase, but the *Ranger* managed to escape—at least temporarily—and anchored at Sullivan's Island.

"It was now learned," Andrew wrote in his memoirs, "that the enemy planned an attack on Charleston. The harbor was completely blockaded, and the ships at the bar were soon joined by others."

The British had tried once before to take control of Charleston, South Carolina. Back in June 1776 American cannon fire from forts on Sullivan's and James Islands had killed more than sixty Royal Navy sailors and wounded more than 130. "No slaughter-house could present so bad a sight," one British officer said.

By the end of 1779, Sir Henry Clinton, commander in chief of the British army in North America, was ready and determined to settle the score.

Andrew and his comrades aboard the *Ranger* did what they could to help defend Charleston. "At the commencement of the cannonading, I was exceeding alarmed," he wrote in his memoirs, "but was careful to conceal my fears from my shipmates. After we had discharged a few broadsides, my fears pretty much subsided, and I, with high spirits, carried cartridges to my gun until the firing ceased."

His confidence was premature. A twenty-four-pound ball lodged in the *Ranger*'s side, near where Andrew stood. "It struck the salt marsh, which deadened its force," he recalled, "or it must have gone through the ship and would have killed me."

The British persisted. When there was no longer any point in remaining onboard, Andrew and the rest of Captain Simpson's crew removed themselves to Fort Gadsden.

Clinton took control of Charleston on May 12, 1780. It was soon discovered that many of the British soldiers had smallpox. American officers quickly ordered inoculations for their men. This involved infecting an individual with a tiny amount of fluid from a smallpox pustule placed in a small incision or puncture wound, usually on the upper arm. The recipient would then get a (hopefully) mild case of the disease, thus building his resistance. "When the symptoms came on, I was greatly alarmed," Andrew reported later, "but I had them very favorably."

As part of the terms of surrender, Andrew and his shipmates were allowed to leave Charleston. They traveled to Newport, Rhode Island. En route many became sick from contaminated water. In Newport, because they had been exposed to smallpox, they had to be thoroughly cleansed in smokehouses set up for the purpose.

"Watched by police officers, we entered one, unpacked our clothes and scattered them all about," Andrew wrote in his memoirs. "We almost suffocated from a smoke made of oakum and tobacco before we were allowed to leave. We then went to a creek to wash."

After making his way from Newport to Boston, Andrew received sad news from a friend of his grandmother: His father had died. Still sick from the bad water he had consumed onboard the ship, Andrew traveled about 60 miles to Portsmouth, where he arrived exhausted and weak from dysentery. Two of the Sherburnes' children were still living with Andrew's mother, who was trying to support them by spinning, knitting, and sewing for others. "She would sit at her wheel for hours without uttering a word," Andrew recalled, "while now and then the tears would roll down her cheeks."

Andrew spent two months at home, recovering from his illness. In December 1780, at the age of fifteen, he set sail again, this time on the *Alexander*, since the *Ranger* had fallen into the hands of the enemy. After a fruitless three-month cruise, Andrew signed on as a crew member of the *Greyhound*, a privately owned ship sailing under the auspices of the United States. Small vessels like the *Greyhound* often had as much success as larger ones. They were quicker and more maneuverable, which came in handy when pursuing or fleeing the enemy.

"Once on board, I found a jovial company," Andrew later recalled. In addition to the usual complement of officers and seamen, the crew included "twenty and thirty boys, scarcely one of them as large as myself and some of them not a dozen years old."

Desperate for recruits, the officers of the *Greyhound* entertained Andrew and the other prospects royally. Andrew enjoyed himself, but once at sea, he was filled with "fearful forebodings." At one point a British ship chased the *Greyhound* but, to Andrew's relief, lost it in the fog. The *Greyhound* failed to take any prizes. The captain and several of the crew, including Andrew, switched boats in Fortune Bay in Newfoundland and set out for Salem, Massachusetts.

A few days later Andrew noticed the captain behaving strangely. The man seemed to think he was back on the *Greyhound*. He would talk to other officers and reply as if they answered him. One morning Andrew and another sailor found the captain's clothes lying on the deck, but the captain was nowhere in sight. Although the crew searched on ship and on land, they never found him.

The voyage seemed even more frightening without a leader. Andrew feared for his life as the ship was tossed about by a storm. He survived the gale only to face terror again when an enemy schooner began to fire on his ship, blowing a hole through the mainsail.

"In a few minutes they were along side of us, and twenty men sprang on board with long guns in their hands, loaded, cocked, and primed. . . . They seemed determined to take our lives." Fortunately for Andrew, the enemy commander interceded.

However, Andrew and his crewmates were sent to prison in Placentia, Newfoundland. In the fall of 1781, it was decided that they should be taken by boat to St. John's, where other prisoners were being held. They had been at sea for about three days when the winds suddenly increased. In the ensuing storm the ship struck a bluff of rocks with such force that the rudder was broken off.

"I was going up the fore hatchway when the ship struck," Andrew recalled. "I gained the quarter-deck where a most terrifying scene was presented to my view. The sea was breaking feather white all around us, and the rain descended in torrents. Some of the officers were raving and swearing. Others were crying and praying."

There seemed to be no way to escape. Swimming to shore was out of the question. Staying alive on the broken pieces of the ship would be nearly impossible. Against enormous odds, two men made it to shore by jumping on rocks. They managed to tie a rope to the spar, part of the ship's rigging.

Andrew watched as a sailor attempted to pull himself along the rope. "He appeared to do well until he got about two rods from the ship," he recorded later in his memoirs, "where he was washed off the rope."

A second man suffered the same fate. Finally, a third man succeeded in getting to shore. After ten men had reached dry ground (four having been washed off the rope), Andrew decided to give it a try.

"The first wave . . . buried me for a short time," he recalled. "When the second wave came, I was exposed to its whole violence. I was stretched out straight horizontally, as if I had been suspended in air."

His right hand gave way. He could feel his left hand slipping.

"I expected to be immediately in eternity," he wrote, "but the undertow swept me beneath the rope."

A third wave swept over him, but by then he could almost touch the rocks below with the tips of his toes. As he floated on another wave, the men on shore reached for him and pulled him in. Andrew was alive, but he was still a prisoner.

After serving for a time on a British vessel, Andrew and his friend Willis announced that they would rather be in jail than continue to help the enemy. Their request was granted.

"We felt ready to leap for joy," Andrew recalled years later. "We were to have the honor and privilege of going to prison."

In November 1781, Andrew and Willis took up residence in Mill Prison in Plymouth, England. Because England had not officially recognized America as a nation, prisoners were charged with treason or piracy and treated as criminals. They could not be exchanged or given any of the privileges normally given to prisoners of war.

Andrew soon discovered other New Hampshire natives in the Mill. He knew one of them personally—Mr. Tibbits, who offered to act as his teacher while they were confined.

"Although I had never had six months' schooling in my life," Andrew later wrote. "I could read tolerably well. However, I could not write my name or enumerate three figures."

Thanks to Mr. Tibbits, the sixteen-year-old made rapid progress in his studies. He got used to prison life, later commenting that the food was "pretty good" though there was not enough of it.

"Miniature ship-building was the most extensive business which was carried on," he wrote. "Sloops of war, frigates, two-deckers, and even three-deckers were built here and sold to local boys whose curiosity led them to take a peep at the Yankees."

By the time spring 1782 arrived, many of the prisoners were sick. Grateful for their kindness to him, Andrew devoted himself to caring for them. Then, one morning, he woke up with a terrible headache. "I rose up . . . but my sight left me," he recalled. "I was almost entirely deranged for several weeks. When my reason returned, I discovered that I was exceedingly weak, and when I began to mend, I did so very slowly."

Andrew and his fellow prisoners were released that same spring. Lord Cornwallis had surrendered at Yorktown back in October 1781, and peace negotiations were under way. Walking poorly "even with two canes," Andrew was helped onto a ship bound for America. He returned to Portsmouth, where he regained his strength. As soon as he felt well enough, he went back to sea to earn a living. Captured by the British again, he was confined aboard the *Jersey* prison ship under the most abominable conditions imaginable.

He fell sick again in January 1783 and was transferred to a

hospital ship. Conditions there were scarcely an improvement. The ordeal left him with a permanently damaged left leg and poor circulation.

After his release in 1783, at age twenty, he took up teaching, supplementing his income as a surveyor. His interest in religion grew, and he eventually became a Baptist minister. During the War of 1812, he served as a military chaplain.

Andrew's first wife, Jane Muchamore, died in 1815. The couple had two children, John and Betsy. Andrew later married Betsy Miller, with whom he had four children: Andrew, Samuel, Mary Jane, and Eliza Ann.

Andrew Sherburne's memoirs were published in 1828. He died in Augusta, New York, in 1831. Born during the early days of American unrest, he served at sea through years of bitter fighting, and at last stood proudly on the soil of a free and independent country.

NO SAFETY FOR YOU HERE

Mary Hunt Palmer

1775–1866

Whenever Mary Palmer's mother told the story, people leaned forward and listened carefully to every word. "On the night of the eighteenth of April, I heard the drum beat," Elizabeth Palmer would say, her eyes bright with the recollection. "I waked Mr. Palmer and said, 'My dear, I hear the drum.' He was out of bed with the rapidity of a bullet from a gun and, while he was dressing, his father entered and said, 'My son, we must ride, I have received an express. Three men lie dead at Lexington.'"

Here Mrs. Palmer might explain that her father-in-law, Joseph Palmer, was a commander in the Massachusetts militia. The listener would nod, picturing the scene that fateful day in April 1775: the militia gathered on the Lexington green; the harsh voice of Maj. John Pitcairn of the Royal Marines, demanding that the rebels lay down their weapons; the battle that left a total of eight American militiamen dead and ten wounded. The British had headed for Concord next, accompanied by the fife's trill and the rumble of the drum.

Joseph Pearse Palmer had given his wife instructions. "Bessy,

Courtesy of the Vermont Historical Society

Mary (Hunt) Palmer Tyler

you must take up the children and fly to some of the back towns. There is no safety for you here."

"Where shall we go?" Mrs. Palmer asked.

Her husband turned to a servant. "John, get the chaise ready to take the children to Newton." To his wife, he said, "Your friend, Mrs. Pigeon, will give you shelter until this alarm is over."

Mrs. Palmer reached into the cradle and straightened her baby's padded leather cap, or "puddinghead cap," designed to protect an infant's fontanel, or soft spot. She wrapped the little girl in a shawl and picked her up. A friend who was visiting took charge of Mrs. Palmer's two-year-old son. The women and children rode a couple of miles by carriage from Watertown to Newton, which was located on a bend of the Charles River, 12 miles from Concord.

"We soon arrived safely at Mr. Pigeon's," Mrs. Palmer would always say, continuing the story. "But lo, and behold! The family, alarmed by the rumors flying about, had fled farther back into the country, leaving their doors open, as was customary then."

Mrs. Palmer and her friend were quickly put to work. "Men with guns in their hands were running in all directions, and some officers, who were trying to organize them a little, called upon us and urged us to have something cooked for the poor fellows who should survive this day."

As Mrs. Palmer prepared the pork, beef, and vegetables she found in the Pigeons' kitchen, she could not help worrying about her husband and her father-in-law. While the food cooked, she and her friend gathered garments, tablecloths, and towels. These they tore up for use as bandages.

Before too long, the survivors of the battle at Concord began to arrive. Hungry, dirty, and exhausted, some crumpled to the floor, unable to stand any longer.

"We beat the rascals," one of them said, referring to the British, "and have driven them back to Boston."

"But my father and husband, where are they?" Mrs. Palmer asked.

"Oh, they have had a dreadful fatiguing day, but they must be here soon," was the answer.

It was ten o'clock at night when the two men rode up to the Pigeons' house. Mrs. Palmer's father-in-law "had to be lifted from his horse and was borne into the house and laid on the parlor floor. It was many hours, under the most judicious treatment, before he showed any encouraging signs of animation."

"Nor was my husband so much better off," Mrs. Palmer related. "They had both been in the saddle from daylight till then, riding all the time."

At last the listener would relax a bit and settle back in his chair, relieved that the women and babies had remained safe. Young Mary Palmer would stand at her mother's elbow, her heart beating. This was the part of the story she liked best—the moment where her mother turned toward her and said: "This little girl was five or six weeks old that morning."

Mary always felt a shiver of importance at the words. She had been that baby, helpless and small, carried off to Newton for safekeeping. Of course she could not remember the incident, yet by the time she was old enough to understand what had happened, it had become part of who she was.

Mary Hunt Palmer was born on March 1, 1775. Her older brother, Joseph, was the toddler who was whisked away to Newton with Mary on April 19. As it turned out, the fighting at Lexington and Concord was only the beginning of what would be a long, bitter war.

In June, when Mary was three months old, British and American forces met at Breed's Hill near Charlestown. Her family's physician, Dr. Joseph Warren, lost his life that day. A member of the Massachusetts committee of safety, Warren had sent Paul Revere on his famous ride to Lexington and Concord on the night of April 18. He had also written a popular song to the tune of "British Grenadiers." Warren's version, called "Free America," included the lyrics:

> Lift up your hearts, my heroes,
> And swear with proud disdain,
> The wretch that would ensnare you
> Shall spread his net in vain;
> Should Europe empty all her force,
> We'd meet them in array,

And shout huzza, huzza, huzza
For brave America.

As Mary grew older, she no doubt heard her mother talk about other family friends such as John and Abigail Adams. Adams later became America's second president.

"There was a distant connection by marriage between our family and the Adams,'" Mrs. Palmer wrote in her memoirs, describing a close social connection. "We lived in the same town, went to the same meeting [church] and used to dine at the old president's house on Sundays."

Although Mary was too young to pay any attention to the battle at Breed's Hill, the Adams' son, John Quincy, nearly eight at the time, was old enough. His mother took him to Penn's Hill to watch the battle from a distance. He never forgot the smoke and flames, the roaring cannons—the tears in his mother's eyes and his own. His early feelings of loyalty to America grew into a long-lasting commitment. As an adult, he served as America's sixth president.

In July 1775 George Washington took command of the American forces besieging the British in Boston. That fall the Palmers relocated to Germantown, Massachusetts, where Mrs. Palmer's father had established a glass works about twenty years earlier with the help of German workers.

Soon after Mary's first birthday, in March 1776, the British ended their defense of Boston. Mrs. Palmer recalled hearing "the cannon from Dorchester Heights" and watching as the British ships left the harbor. In July the Declaration of Independence was read aloud to excited crowds all across the land.

Some of Mary's earliest memories were of playing with her brother, Joseph, at Germantown. The Palmers' second daughter, Elizabeth, was born in 1778, when Mary was three. That same year, Benjamin Franklin negotiated an alliance between France and America.

The Palmer children spent much of their time scampering through a large stone house abandoned by the Germans who had once lived there. In *Grandmother Tyler's Book*, Mary's memoirs written when she was in her eighties, she wrote: "There was a tradition that the first owners had quarreled and fought, and that someone was killed among them, and that consequently the premises were haunted."

Mary and her brother could not imagine visiting the house after dark, but they explored every corner by daylight. Joe's favorite activity was sliding down the banister. He would not allow Mary to imitate him, however, because girls "should not climb in such dangerous places."

Before long, little sister Bessy was old enough to join Joe and Mary in their games of leapfrog, hide and seek, and hopscotch. They were under no immediate threat from British soldiers, but they managed to put themselves in harm's way nonetheless. One day in particular, the sea turned into a formidable enemy.

"Another pastime we were very fond of was wading at low tide out upon the little sand hills which were left bare, to pick up shells," Mary recalled. "We were for years in the habit of doing this, and procuring beautiful shells which we would send to our cousins in the interior."

On the day in question, Joe, Mary, and Bessy waded a bit farther than usual. At a distance they saw a little island covered with seaweed and shells. Eager to add to their collection, the children "pressed forward to get them." Busy gathering shells in their aprons, they paid no attention to the rising water. "At length, to our dismay, we found our island grew smaller and smaller, and looking around could not discern the way we came; the water was over our knees on every side."

To make matters worse, stormy winds began to blow. "Dark clouds were in the west and it began to thunder and lighten," Mary wrote later. "Such screaming we set up was a caution. Fortunately, my father was at home and from the parlor window could see our danger."

Shedding boots and stockings, Mr. Palmer waded out to their rescue. He hoisted a daughter under each arm and told Joe to follow him. "We were more careful in the future," Mary wrote. "But often at this day, when I think how those waves rolled and how fast our ground vanished beneath our feet, my heart beats up."

The time spent in Germantown "was the happiest portion of my mother's life," Mary recalled. "Quite retired from the noise and strife of war, she devoted her time to the education of her little ones."

Of course the war was never completely forgotten. When the children misbehaved, their Aunt Sally frightened them by saying she would have "the Regulars" come and get them. This reference to the British troops always had the desired effect.

Mary and her siblings received their daily lessons in their mother's room, a cheerful chamber with a scrubbed white pine floor and white muslin bed and window curtains. The room overlooked the ocean. Typically when the children looked out, they saw gulls and other seabirds or perhaps a dolphin or two leaping among the waves. On one occasion, however, they saw something that filled them with dread. Mary described the incident years later: "Suddenly our attention was attracted and all our fears aroused by the appearance of a splendid barge crowded with gaily decked officers with their cocked hats and shining epaulettes, just coming around a point of land which we all knew was on the way to Boston."

Joseph, Mary, and Bessy feared that Aunt Sally had finally made good her threat and summoned the Regulars. "We . . . began an outcry," Mary recalled, "some running up [to the] garret and some clinging to mother in great terror."

Mrs. Palmer calmed the children, assuring them that the men were not British but French. Mr. Palmer invited them into the house and from that point on, French soldiers were indeed "regulars" at the Palmers.

"Once we had an officer boarding with us many weeks," Mary wrote. "He had been wounded and was still quite an invalid. . . .

He used to play the flute and sing with my father."

In February 1780 the Palmers welcomed another child into the family with the birth of John Hampden, and that same year the family moved to Boston. By then Spain had joined America and France in the war against the British. Fighting had intensified in the South. The British had control of Savannah, Georgia, and on May 12, 1780, Charleston, South Carolina, fell to His Majesty's troops. A week later, Mary and everyone else in New England forgot about the war—at least for a moment.

Mrs. Palmer was expecting guests for dinner. To get Mary and her little sister out from underfoot, she sent them down the lane to school. "She dressed us both in our best, ready to see the company," Mary related. "I remember our pink frocks and red morocco shoes and white stockings . . . So we went, I leading the little one, then two years old."

Mary herself was only five years old and had never been to school before. In fact, when she was naughty, she was "often threatened with being sent to school." She and Bessy soon arrived at the home of "an aged matron, who taught a school of little folks." All was well until midmorning, when the sky suddenly began to grow dark. At first everyone thought it was about to rain, and Mary wondered how she was going to get home without ruining her new shoes.

"It grew darker and darker, so that at last the mistress said we might go home as we could not see to read. There was a great hurrying, you may be sure, for although the old lady tried not to frighten us, it was very evident she was frightened herself."

Soot-colored rain was falling. Unable to see in the dark, Mary plunged into a gutter designed to carry waste water from the house. Her clothes and shoes were spattered with filth. She was not alone in her terror. People throughout New England were in a panic. Many of them thought "the consummation of all things was at hand."

Mary's father did not accept that explanation. According to

Mary, he said "that the smell of smoke and the burnt leaves flying in the air plainly told the cause, in addition to a dense fog, which hung about the coast for several days before and continued." Mr. Palmer was right. "The dark day," as it came to be known, was caused by smoke from numerous forest fires in New York and Canada.

Mrs. Palmer continued her children's education at home. The textbooks of the day included spellers, grammars, readers, and "arithmetickers." "Bessy and I learnt with comparative ease," Mary recalled. "Joseph liked figures better than poetry and excelled us on the slate."

The book they used was *The New England Primer*, an essentially religious text. To learn the alphabet, children memorized such verses as "In Adam's fall, we sinned all" and "Heaven to find; the Bible mind." Even in her old age, Mary remembered the lines written by Isaac Watts against quarreling and fighting:

Let dogs delight to bark and bite
For God has made them so:
Let bears and lions growl and fight,
For 'tis their nature, too.

But, children, you should never let
Such angry passions rise:
Your little hands were never made
To tear each other's eyes.

For Mary and Bessy, education also included learning to sew and embroider as well as other homemaking skills. These were considered more important to their future than knowledge found in books.

On September 3, 1782, the Palmers' fifth child was born—a son, Edward. By then peace negotiations were under way in Paris. A peace treaty was drafted by November 5, wherein Great Britain agreed to recognize American independence and evacuate all

British troops. Mary's mother soon had another story to tell, this one guaranteed to bring a smile to the listener's face.

"In January 1783, my children were playing on the floor and I was busy at work, when in came my husband in a great gale; he danced about the room, taking hornpipe steps for which he was famous, and clapped his hands, and seized Mary in his arms, and jumped her about with every demonstration of joy."

Mary's recollection was similar: "Mother sat at her work-table as usual. She sprang up exclaiming, 'Mr. Palmer, what is the matter? What does ail you?' He dropped me instantly, clasped her in his arms, flew around the room kissing her over and over again and at last exclaimed 'Peace is declared! Hurrah!'"

After the war, Mr. and Mrs. Palmer had four more children: Amelia, Sophia, George, and Catherine Hunt.

When Mary was just eight or nine years old she encountered her husband-to-be. Royall Tyler was a lawyer in his twenties who had come to visit the Palmers. Mary was enchanted by the young man from the very beginning and later wrote: "I was astonished; his appearance, his manners, his looks overpowered me; I had never seen anything so beautiful I thought."

When Mary was nineteen, in 1794, the two married and settled in Vermont. They had eleven children: Royall, John Steele, Mary Whitwell, Edward Royall, William Clark, Joseph Dennie, Amelia Sophia, George Palmer, (Charles) Royall, Thomas Pickman, and Abiel Winship.

Royall Tyler was not only a lawyer but also author of *The Contrast*, a satirical play performed in New York, Philadelphia, Baltimore, and Boston. The play contrasted the simple honesty of American life with what Tyler perceived as the hypocritical, artificial society life practiced abroad. Tyler also wrote other prose, poetry, and plays.

Mary eventually saw her name in print as well. Her book *The Maternal Physician* was published in 1811. The title page described the volume as "A Treatise on the Nurture and Management of Infants, from the Birth until Two Years Old. Being the Result of Sixteen Years' Experience in the Nursery, Illustrated by Extracts from the Most Approved Medical Authors. By an American Matron." Mary dedicated the book to her mother, writing: "That helpless babe which reposed on your affrighted bosom when you fled the vicinity of Boston, on the day of the ever memorable battle of Lexington, now a wife, a mother, and near the meridian of life, as a small tribute for all your maternal cares, most respectfully addresses this little volume to your perusal; candidly confessing that all which is valuable in it she derived from you."

One of the most famous literary talents in Mary's family was the man her niece Sophia married. He was Nathaniel Hawthorne, author of *The Scarlet Letter, The House of Seven Gables*, and other classics.

Mary Hunt Palmer Tyler penned her final entry in *Grandmother Tyler's Book* in November 1863. "If I should attempt to record all the incidents and events of the last fifty years of my life," she wrote, "my strength and your patience would be exhausted; therefore I bid you adieu."

During her life she saw "the birth of the American Nation" as well as the war between that nation's northern and southern states. She died on July 7, 1866, in Brattleboro, Vermont, at age ninety-one. On her tombstone in the cemetery on Prospect Hill, her sons and daughters inscribed the familiar Biblical words: "And her children rise up and call her blessed."

WORTHY OF THE PRAISE

James Durham

1762–?

By the time James Durham reached his thirteenth birthday, on May 1, 1775, he was keenly aware of what slavery meant. He knew it was different from being an indentured servant or apprentice. Boys who were servants or apprentices would one day be released. That was not likely to happen to James, one of approximately 550,000 slaves in America at the time.

Nothing is known of James's life before 1775. When he was in his twenties, he told renowned physician Benjamin Rush a little about his teenage years, starting with the fact that he was once owned by Dr. John Kearsley Jr.

Kearsley, a prominent Philadelphia physician, had cofounded the Philadelphia Medical Society. He was considered an expert on what was called "angina maligna," or "putrid sore throat"—most likely diphtheria. Kearsley taught James to mix drugs and trained him to assist in the treatment of patients.

In 1775 America and England went to war, and life in the Kearsley household took a disturbing turn. Dr. Kearsley was a Loyalist. Outspoken and quick tempered, he proclaimed his allegiance to the king of England at every opportunity and argued hotly with those who disagreed. Before long, the doctor's opinions and actions dramatically changed the lives of everyone around him, including James's.

One afternoon in early September, Kearsley heard shouting outside his elegant home just below High Street. Looking out, he saw about thirty people in the street. In a cart sat Isaac Hunt, a lawyer who had recently defended a man who refused to boycott British goods. Anti-British colonists were hauling Hunt around town in a cart, accompanied by fife and drum. They stopped at intervals to allow Hunt to apologize in a loud voice for sympathizing with the Crown.

The sight infuriated Kearsley. He had noticed that attacks were becoming more and more common on Loyalists—or "Tories" as the rebellious Whigs called him and those who shared his views. As Kearsley watched the performance in the street, his anger mounted. He would not stand by and let a respectable citizen be treated in such a manner. He reached for his pistol.

The bang from Kearsley's gun was not "the shot heard round the world." That had been fired at Lexington, Massachusetts, in April. Kearsley's shot did, however, get the attention of the crowd outside his home. As Kearsley's slave, James may or may not have seen what happened next, but he certainly would have heard about it later. Christopher Marshall, a Philadelphia pharmacist, recorded the incident in his diary on September 6, 1775. "They seized him," he wrote, referring to Kearsley. "[And] took his pistol. In the scuffle, he got wounded in the hand. They then took Hunt out of the cart . . . put Kearsley in, brought him to the Coffee House."

Quaker Elizabeth Drinker also reported the episode in her diary, commenting that the doctor's hand was "much wounded with a Bayonet."

Unlike Hunt, Kearsley refused to apologize for his actions. According to a bystander named Graydon: "The doctor, foaming with rage and indignation, without a hat, his wig dishevelled, and himself bloody from his wounded hand, stood up in the cart and called for a bowl of punch; when so vehement was his thirst that he swallowed it all ere he took it from his lips."

“I was shocked at the spectacle,” Graydon said. “Thus to see a lately respected citizen so vilified.”

When the mob shouted “huzza!” Kearsley swung his wig around his head and yelled even louder to show his contempt. Marshall’s diary entry continued: “They then, with drum beating, paraded the streets round the town, then took him back to his house and left him there. The mob . . . then broke the windows and abused the house, etc.”

One can only imagine the reaction of Kearsley’s wife and children, as well as James and the other slaves and servants. They must have been not only shocked but also terrified as glass shattered around them.

The “Tory doctor,” as Kearsley came to be called, had been lucky in a way. He had escaped the more severe types of punishment sometimes given to his kind. Loyalists had, on occasion, been whipped or beaten. Some had been “tarred and feathered,” which involved pouring hot tar over the offender and then covering him with feathers. A ride through town on a wooden rail might follow, which often caused serious injuries.

James did not record his reaction to the wrath of the patriot crowd and his master’s humiliation. He probably hoped nothing more would come of the matter. Unfortunately Kearsley’s troubles were just beginning.

On October 6, 1775, the *Constitutional Gazette* reported: “The infamous Dr. Kearsley of Philadelphia, not content with his late triumphal procession for his enmity to this country, has made a further attempt to injure it, but to-day was happily discovered. Some letters of his were intercepted in a vessel bound from here to London.”

Kearsley and two other men were seized by the local Committee of Safety. In his diary Christopher Marshall described the confiscated letters as “base and cruel invectives against the liberties of America, and calculated by wicked men to inflame the minds of the people in England against the Colonies in general.” The letters also contained a map of the Delaware channel and other important military information.

Once again Kearsley showed no remorse for his actions. Once again he narrowly escaped being tarred and feathered. He was locked up in the local prison, his office was sealed, and a guard was placed at his house. On October 24 he was moved from Philadelphia to Lancaster, and his family was left to adjust to his absence as best they could.

In spring 1776, Kearsley was expelled by St. George's Society, a charitable and social organization. The announcement, published in the *Pennsylvania Gazette* on March 6, stated that the doctor had "shown himself inimical to the Liberties of this Country, and therefore rendered himself unworthy of being a Member of this Society." Seven months later, the Committee of Safety at Philadelphia transferred Kearsley to a jail in Carlisle. Their report described him as "a dangerous Enemy to the American States."

Meanwhile, the American Congress had issued its Declaration of Independence. "We hold these Truths to be self-evident," it stated, "that all Men are created equal."

Like many other slaves of his day, James Durham must have wondered if a patriot victory would bring an end to slavery in America. He could only hope that would be the case. For now, however, he was at the mercy of his master. With Kearsley in prison, James's fate was uncertain.

Loyalists accused of crimes were usually housed in filthy, rundown prisons in the back country. Kearsley was not suited to such a life, and some say he went mad at Carlisle. In any case, he died there in November 1777, survived by his wife and five children.

Sometime between Kearsley's arrest and death, James Durham was sold. According to information given to Benjamin Rush years later, James "passed through several hands," eventually becoming the property of Dr. West, a surgeon in the Sixteenth British Regiment.

England's Sixteenth Regiment of Foot had arrived in New York back in 1767 and was ordered to various southern posts. In August 1776 a detachment returned to New York but was sent back to the south the following year. West may have purchased James Durham during that time and taken the fifteen-year-old south.

The practice of medicine in the British army differed from what James had encountered in Dr. Kearsley's office. Some regiments had licensed physicians on staff, but many did not. Army surgeons were not required to have a medical degree and they were poorly paid. Surgeons were given money to purchase medicine and other supplies and were allowed to keep any surplus for themselves, which encouraged them to cut costs. Not surprisingly, their patients often paid a price.

Surgeons' mates, or assistants, were not tested on their medical knowledge. Yet, in the absence of a physician or surgeon, a surgeon's mate could shoulder full responsibility for a regiment's medical care. West was probably thrilled to have James. After all, the boy had experience!

The typical British soldier may or may not have been healthy when he enlisted, but after he did, many factors worked against his remaining or becoming healthy. A soldier's diet was neither balanced nor nutritious. Clothing was inappropriate or insufficient, or both. The men were crowded together in ships or camps, an ideal environment for diseases to spread.

James and his new master had to treat various disabling ailments, including dysentery, lung disorders, scurvy, and typhoid fever. James was exposed to all of these, and he may well have suffered from more than one himself.

In September 1779, the Sixteenth Regiment of Foot came to the defense of British-held forts at Baton Rouge, Louisiana. By then Spain had declared war on Britain. Patriot troops at Baton Rouge included Creoles, Native Americans, African Americans, and Spanish regulars organized by Louisiana's Spanish governor, Don Bernardo de Galvez. The British lost the Battle of Baton Rouge, and James received on-the-job training in treating the horrific injuries inflicted by muskets, bayonets, and cannons.

In the spring of 1781, the Sixteenth Regiment fought at Pensacola, Florida. This time Galvez and his troops were assisted by several French frigates and a Spanish fleet, and the British surrendered to Galvez on May 10.

That October, when the war ended, James was sold to Dr. Robert Dow (sometimes written as Dove) of New Orleans, under whom the nineteen-year-old's medical education continued.

Great Britain officially recognized the independence of the United States in the Treaty of Paris on September 3, 1783. That same year James purchased his freedom from Dow for five hundred pesos "upon easy terms." He was twenty-one years old.

With Dow's help, James set up a small medical practice. At the outbreak of the Revolution, university-educated physicians were not common in America. Only about 5 percent of American physicians had medical degrees. Apprentice-trained practitioners were the norm, and James had years of training under three physicians.

In 1788 James traveled to Philadelphia, where he was baptized into the Episcopal Church and met physician Benjamin Rush, a signer of the Declaration of Independence. Dr. Rush introduced James to prominent Philadelphia physicians William Shippen Jr., John Redman, and Adam Kuhn. Rush was so impressed with James that he shared the young man's story with the Pennsylvania Abolition Society in a public statement on November 14, 1788: "I have conversed with him upon most of the acute and epidemic diseases of the country where he lives, and was pleased to find him perfectly acquainted with the modern simple mode of practice in those diseases. . . . He is very modest and engaging in his manners. He speaks French fluently and has some knowledge of the Spanish language."

After returning to New Orleans, James corresponded with Rush for more than a dozen years. In a letter dated May 29, 1789, James wrote: "Gratitude, duty and view of future advantages, all contribute to make me thoroughly sensible how much I ought to labour for my own improvement and your satisfaction, and to show myself worthy of the praise and honours that you have taken of me [sic]."

In 1794 James wrote to Rush asking for his "treatise of the yellow fever." Explaining that the disease was "very bad among the English," he went on to say that he had treated fifty yellow-fever patients and lost only six, "less than all the other doctors here."

In 1801 Spanish authorities in New Orleans ordered five practitioners to close their offices until they received licenses to practice medicine. Mention was made of a "free Negro Derum," stating that he would have "the right only to cure throat disease and no other." It seems likely that this was a reference to James Durham, whose first mentor, Dr. John Kearsley Jr., specialized in "putrid sore throat."

Unfortunately, researchers have been unable to find any other records indicating that James was a doctor in New Orleans. He is not listed in the New Orleans city directories for 1805 or 1822. Some assert that his story is largely a myth; others disagree. According to Charles E. Wynes of the University of Georgia, "The mystery remains, but so does the record of this 'first black physician' in America, together with that of the uncommon friendship between one of America's most distinguished figures and a former slave."

The last trace that historians have found of James Durham is a letter to Rush dated April 5, 1802. In it, James asks Rush for a pamphlet on "the pox" and thanks him for "the three pamphlets you were so good as to send me."

Did James leave New Orleans when the authorities limited his scope of practice to "throat disease"? Did he die from illness or a fatal accident before 1805? Both of these possibilities would explain his absence from city directories. The latter would explain why no other communication with Rush has been found.

Although these questions remain unanswered, James Durham's accomplishments are heralded even today. Clinton Cox wrote in his book *African American Healers*, published in 2000: "Despite [James Durham's] achievements, the idea that black people were incapable of understanding medicine remained widespread in the decades to come. In the face of often incredible odds, however, many African-American men and women wrote their names into history as outstanding doctors, nurses, and researchers."

James Durham, slave of "the Tory doctor," is part of this legacy.

A SPIRIT WARM AND BOLD

Deborah Samson

1760–1827

In the fall of 1768, British troops arrived in Boston, Massachusetts. Even though England and America were not at war, Royal Governor Thomas Gage had requested military assistance. The people of Boston had him worried.

"They seem to me in an actual state of rebellion," he declared in September. "I am taking measures to defeat any treasonable designs."

Bostonians were less than thrilled with their uninvited guests, and the guests knew it. "The arrival of his Majesty's troops in Boston was extremely obnoxious to its inhabitants," commented Thomas Preston, a British captain stationed in the town.

His words were an understatement. By the spring of 1770, brawls between citizens and soldiers were common. Each act of violence spawned more violence. Then, on the cold, snow-covered night of March 5, the town went crazy.

According to the *Boston Gazette and Country Journal*, at about nine o'clock two boys were walking past a narrow alley leading to a barracks. There they saw "a soldier brandishing a broad sword of an uncommon size against the walls, out of which he struck fire plentifully." With him was "a person of mean countenance armed

Courtesy of the Rhode Island Historical Society

Portrait of Deborah Samson (Gannett), 1797
oil on panel by Joseph Stone

with a large cudgel." A fight ensued between the boys and the two British soldiers, and "the noise brought people together."

To be exact, it brought about 400 townspeople together. They threw snowballs and chunks of ice at the soldiers. The army rallied to protect its own, threatening to run the civilians through with bayonets. The crowd waved clubs and knives and taunted the men, daring them to fire. In the confusion, soldiers began shooting.

Five citizens were killed in the incident. Patriot Samuel Adams called it a "massacre," hoping to fan the flame of rebellion. His effort did not succeed, at least not right away. A Boston court accepted a plea of self-defense from five of the soldiers. Two others were branded on the thumb as punishment and discharged from the military. All parties seemed to feel justice had been done.

About 50 miles south, in the town of Middleborough, ten-year-old Deborah Samson heard about the "Boston Massacre." She understood that something terrible had happened, yet the troubles in Boston did not seem to affect her personally. She had no way of knowing that the conflict between England and America would escalate, resulting in more bloodshed—and that some of that blood would be her own.

Since the age of eight, Deborah had lived in Middleborough with an elderly widow named Mrs. Thatcher. At first the little girl's duties had been fairly light. Lately, however, she had been asked to take on more strenuous jobs such as hauling water, washing clothes, scrubbing pots, and tossing out the garbage, or slops. Deborah's mother had recently decided these tasks were too demanding for a child and had told Deborah she would find her a more suitable position. Deborah was not sure she wanted to move again so soon. She had already moved twice in the past five years.

Born in Plympton, Massachusetts, on December 17, 1760, Deborah Samson was the fifth child of Jonathan and Deborah Bradford Samson. She had an older sister, Hannah, and three older brothers—Jonathan, Elisha, and Ephraim. When she was four years old, her brother Nehemiah was born.

On her mother's side, Deborah was a descendant of William Bradford, first governor of the Plymouth Colony. Her father's ancestors included *Mayflower* passengers John and Priscilla Alden and Miles Standish. Despite this impressive heritage, the Samsons were far from rich. Their situation grew worse in 1765 when Deborah's father left for England to seek his fortune. Deborah's mother was expecting another child at the time. One day the family received news that Jonathan Samson's ship had been lost in a terrible storm. (Evidence later surfaced that Samson, still very much alive, had relocated to Maine, where he died in 1811.)

Left alone with seven children and in ill health, Deborah's mother turned to relatives for help. She found homes for the older children and kept Nehemiah and Sylvia, the new baby, with her. Deborah was sent to live with Ruth Fuller, her mother's cousin. There the five-year-old had her own room, nice clothes, and good food. She started learning to read.

Unfortunately for Deborah, Ruth Fuller died just three years after taking her in. Reverend Sylvanus Conant of the First Congregational Church in Middleborough suggested that Mrs. Samson consider placing her daughter with Mrs. Thatcher.

Now, at age ten, Deborah had to pack her few belongings and move again. After conferring with Reverend Conant, her mother "bound her out" to Jeremiah Thomas, a member of Conant's church. As was the custom, Mrs. Samson signed a contract promising that Deborah would work for the Thomas family until she was eighteen years old. In exchange, they would provide the girl with life's basic necessities. People had many reasons for becoming indentured servants or "binding themselves out" in colonial days. Some had earned their passage to America that way.

Life with the Thomases was a major change for Deborah. Mr. and Mrs. Thomas and their eight sons lived on a big farm near Middleborough. With such a large family, Mrs. Thomas spent a lot of time cooking, sewing, and weaving, and she was grateful for Deborah's help. The girl also fed the animals and performed other chores around the farm. She especially enjoyed tending the vegetable and herb garden. On occasion, Deborah was allowed to attend school. Usually, however, she studied at home, copying lessons from the Thomas boys' books, which improved her reading skills.

Troubles continued to brew between England and America. In 1771, commencement exercises at Princeton University featured an epic poem by graduating students Philip Freneau and Hugh Henry Brackenridge. Titled "The Rising Glory of America," the poem declared:

> Nor shall these angry tumults here subside
> Nor murder cease, through all these provinces,
> Till foreign crowns have vanished from our view
> And dazzle here no more—no more presume
> To awe the spirit of fair Liberty.

Freneau eventually earned the title "Poet of the Revolution." Little did Deborah know that one day he would write a poem about her.

In May 1773, England passed the Tea Act, which involved collecting taxes on the sale of tea. Seven months later, on the night of December 16, members of a radical group called the Sons of Liberty disguised themselves as Mohawk Indians, boarded British ships in Boston Harbor, and dumped the cargo of tea into the water. Britain retaliated by banning the loading or unloading of any ships in Boston Harbor until the tea was paid for.

This Boston Port Act was supposed to drive a wedge between radical Boston and the rest of America. Instead, the other colonies rallied around Massachusetts. On September 5, 1774, colonial delegates met in Philadelphia to discuss uniting in rebellion against the Crown.

The Boston Tea Party took place the night before Deborah Samson's thirteenth birthday. She understood the seriousness of the event, but it was hard for her to identify with a group of men who dressed up like Indians and destroyed a whole shipment of tea. Besides, she had other concerns: Two more children had been born to the Thomases—both boys—and they required a lot of attention.

At age thirteen, Deborah was a remarkably tall girl, healthy and strong, with blonde hair and blue eyes. The Thomas boys treated her as a sister. They taught her how to shoot a gun and sometimes took her hunting with them. When friends and neighbors talked about a possible war with England, Deborah realized that such a war might affect her personally. People who were dear to her might be killed.

On April 19, 1775, word arrived in Middleborough that colonial militiamen had clashed with British troops at Lexington and Concord, just west of Boston, and war became a reality. The oldest Thomas boys joined the local minutemen—so called because they vowed to be ready to fight at a minute's notice.

That summer the war became even more real to Deborah. On the morning of June 17, she thought she heard thunder booming in the distance. Soon she found out that British ships were cannonading the Charlestown Peninsula, just across the harbor from Boston. The noise continued for hours. That night Deborah learned the details of the fight that would later become known as the Battle of Bunker Hill.

Although the British technically won the battle, more than 40 percent of their troops were wounded or killed. In addition, they had to face the repugnant fact that the undisciplined, outnumbered, and outgunned Americans had made a decent showing against King George III's elite.

In March 1776 American troops under Gen. George Washington forced the British out of Boston. On July 4 the American Congress approved the Declaration of Independence, written by Thomas Jefferson. The document was read aloud in every village and town across America, including Middleborough. Parades were held, accompanied by fife and drum. Military companies marched through the streets.

With mixed emotions, Deborah watched as the men and boys of Middleborough signed up to serve in the army. She was proud yet sad when the Thomas boys and Reverend Conant stepped forward. She knew she might never see them again, but she also envied them a little. What would it be like, the fifteen-year-old girl wondered, to be on your own—to see places you had only heard or read about?

Meanwhile, her role as a female seemed clear. In the absence of husbands, fathers, and sons, the women of Middleborough took on extra duties. In addition to the household tasks they had performed before, they ploughed fields, cut wood, and repaired fences. Even hunting became their responsibility.

Colonial women had increased their spinning and weaving activities before the war started. A boycott of British goods had left colonists with two choices: Make your own or do without. Women had to weave by hand the cloth they had once purchased from England. At the outbreak of the Revolution few soldiers of the Continental army had uniforms; towns were given production quotas to keep the men clothed. A New York teenager declared that although women could not lead the troops, they were "a fighting army of amazones . . . armed with spinning wheels."

On November 16, 1776, the British took Fort Washington, New York. Wounded in the fight was an American woman, Margaret Corbin. She had followed her husband when he enlisted in a Pennsylvania regiment. When Corbin was killed during the battle, his wife took over his gun, and it was rumored that Mrs. Corbin had actually received a soldier's pay. Deborah could only imagine the thrill of living such an exciting life and getting paid besides. She had never had money of her own.

Fighting continued throughout 1777. In February 1778 France formed an alliance with the United States. What had begun as an American bid for independence became a world war.

In December 1778, the British captured Savannah, Georgia, kicking off a major southern campaign. That same month Deborah Samson turned eighteen, and she was no longer bound to the Thomases as their indentured servant. She decided to get a job as a teacher since women were needed to replace schoolmasters who had gone to war.

For two years Deborah taught public school in a village about 2 miles from the Thomas home. Her students learned from several basic textbooks. Primers contained text and rhyming verses that taught students Christian principles as well as how to read. The primer used in Deborah's classroom may have had a picture of King George III on the front. Primers published after the American Revolution featured George Washington and other patriot leaders on the cover instead of the king.

Older children read from the Psalter, or Book of Psalms. They progressed from there to studying the New Testament, followed by the entire Bible. Spelling, writing, and arithmetic were also taught. Children usually shared books because paper was not easily available and printing was expensive.

Like all teachers of the day, Deborah focused on different skills for girls and boys. For example, boys learned to write because they would probably need that skill to get a job. Girls were not expected to have jobs, so it was more important for them to learn to sew than to write. There was no sense in wasting valuable paper to teach girls a craft they would never use.

As the war entered its sixth year, Deborah was twenty years old, as strong as most men and taller than the average man. At this point in her life, she made a radical decision: Dressed in men's clothes, she enlisted in the Continental army, claiming to be Robert Shurtlieff, a fifteen-year-old boy.

Historians and writers have offered several possible explanations for Deborah's actions. Some say she wanted to escape the attentions of a suitor she did not love. Others cite her longing for adventure and travel. Patriotism could have been her motive. Perhaps she wanted to escape the limitations society imposed on women by taking up a weapon other than the spinning wheel.

By the time Deborah signed up, British troops under Gen. Charles Cornwallis had already surrendered to the Americans at Yorktown, Virginia. Even so, fighting continued in many parts of the United States. A bounty receipt dated May 23, 1782, indicates that "Robert Shurtlieff" received the sum of sixty pounds to serve a term of three years.

In the fall of 1782, church leaders at Third Baptist Church, where Deborah was a member, expressed their disapproval of her actions. A document dated September 3 stated that Deborah had "behaved very loose and unChristianlike." In addition she "was accused of dressing in mens cloths and enlisting as a soldier in the army." Apparently Deborah was not convicted of the offense but, the report continued, she "was strongly suspected of being guilty." The church concluded that its duty was to "withhold fellowship until she returns and makes Christian satisfaction."

By then Deborah had made her way to West Point, where she joined the Fourth Massachusetts Regiment. While serving with the Fourth, she was wounded in a skirmish near Tarrytown, New York. In the summer of 1783, Deborah became critically ill and was hospitalized, and a doctor discovered that "Robert Shurtlieff" was a woman.

Deborah was discharged in October at age twenty-two and began teaching school again. Two years later, on April 7, 1785, she married Benjamin Gannett, a farmer from Sharon, Massachusetts. The couple had three children—Earl Bradford, Mary, and Patience. In addition, they took in and raised Susanna Baker Shepard, who was left an orphan when she was five days old.

The Gannetts were not well-off financially. In January 1792, Deborah petitioned the Commonwealth of Massachusetts for a pension. In the petition she explained that she had "made some application to receive pay" for her services, but "being a Female, & not knowing the proper steps to take to get pay . . . has hitherto not received one farthing." The Commonwealth issued Deborah "the sum of Thirty four pounds bearing interest from October 23, 1783."

In 1797, shortly after she turned age thirty-seven, Deborah petitioned the Commonwealth for an "invalid pension," given to soldiers who had become invalids as a result of their military service.

Deborah had never fully recovered from the wound she received in battle. Two of the influential patriots who came forward on her behalf were Philip Freneau and Paul Revere. Freneau composed an ode on her behalf, which included the following verses:

> With the same vigorous soul inspired
> As Joan of Arc, of old,
> With zeal against the Briton fired,
> Her spirit warm and bold.

He urged Congress to give Deborah "something in the wane of days / To make her snug, and keep her warm . . . "

He continued:

> And something to the pocket too,
> Your bounty might afford,
> Of her, who did our foes pursue
> With bayonet, gun, and sword.

Paul Revere wrote to William Eustis, representative from Massachusetts, stating that Deborah "is now much out of health. She has several children, her husband is a good sort of man, tho of small force in business; they have a few acres of poor land which they cultivate, but they are really poor. She told me that no doubt her ill health is in consequence of her being exposed when she did a soldier's duty, and that while in the army she was wounded."

He concluded his letter by saying: "I think her case much more deserving than hundreds to whom Congress has been generous."

Deborah was granted an invalid pension.

In 1802, at the age of forty-one, she defied convention again and toured New England, lecturing on her wartime experiences. Deborah appeared before audiences in a replica of the blue and white uniform she had worn as a Continental soldier. Musket in hand, she demonstrated maneuvers from the manual of arms.

Deborah's first performance took place at the Federal Street Theatre in Boston, following a production of Shakespeare's *King*

Henry IV. In a diary she kept during the tour, Deborah commented on the audience's reaction to her as she sat among them and later, as she delivered her address: "Some of them which I happened to overhear swore that I was a lad of not more than eighteen years of age. . . . I think I may with much candor applaud the people for their serious attention and peculiar respect, especially the ladies."

While on tour, Deborah renewed old acquaintances. In her diary entry for July 10, 1802, she mentions an extended visit with Capt. George Webb, her company commander from the Fourth Massachusetts Regiment.

Deborah lived long enough to enjoy twelve grandchildren, at least one of whom referred to her as "the Old Soldier." She died on April 29, 1827, in Sharon, at the age of sixty-six, and is buried in Rock Ridge Cemetery.

As a child, Deborah must have seen very few options when she tried to imagine her future. In her day, a girl raised in a world of poverty and hard work could usually look forward to more of the same, with a husband and children added in for good measure. She did not foresee the astonishing detour she would take on the way to marriage and motherhood. She never guessed that she would become a larger-than-life legend—the subject of study and discussion not only into the next century but into the next millennium as well.

The earliest known account of Deborah's life was written by Herman Mann in 1797. It was called *The Female Review, or Memoirs of an American Young Lady*. Mann also wrote the speech Deborah delivered on her lecture tour. Many books and articles on Deborah have been published since, most based heavily on Mann's work. Unfortunately, in Mann's zeal to make Deborah into, as scholar Judith Hiltner put it, "a Republican Minerva . . . a model of wisdom, chastity, and courage," he created a legend that all but obscured our understanding of the real Deborah Samson.

Honors accorded Deborah Samson Gannett include giving her name to a Liberty ship launched in Baltimore in 1944. A rose named for Deborah was introduced in 1947, and a park was established in her honor in 1975 in Sharon, Massachusetts. In 1983 Deborah was declared the Official Heroine of the Commonwealth of Massachusetts, and in 1985 the United States Capitol Historical Society issued a commemorative medal in her honor.

Author's Note: Deborah's last name is often spelled "Sampson," but documentary records indicate that "Samson" is correct. In the Federal Census of 1790, Deborah's brother suddenly became a "Sampson." Mann picked up the misspelling in his book, and today its use is quite common. Deborah's alias, "Robert Shurtlieff," is spelled numerous ways in accounts of her life. I have chosen the spelling used in the signature that appears on the bounty receipt from May 1782.

NOT BORN TO BE DROWNED

Ebenezer Fox

1763–1843

To Ebenezer Fox of Roxbury, Massachusetts, one thing was clear: The time had come to right a great wrong. For too long the tyrants had abused their power and imposed their will. Liberty was all that mattered and the sooner the better—no matter what the cost!

Ebenezer was not alone in his convictions that spring of 1775. Patrick Henry, a member of the House of Burgesses in Virginia, stated the position eloquently. "Is life so dear, or peace so sweet, as to be purchased at the price of chains and slavery?" he asked. "Forbid it, Almighty God! I know not what course others may take, but as for me, give me liberty or give me death!"

Although Ebenezer Fox and Patrick Henry were both zealous in their beliefs, there were several differences between the two. Henry was nearly forty years old, and Ebenezer Fox was twelve. Henry was referring to America's rebellion against injustices committed by Great Britain. Ebenezer Fox had his own personal wrongs to right.

Ebenezer's father, Richard Fox, was a tailor and very poor. Richard Fox and his wife, Elizabeth, had a large family. Under such circumstances, children were expected to contribute to their own maintenance early in life. At age seven, Ebenezer had been placed under the care of a neighboring farmer named Pelham.

Farm life was demanding. Tools of the day were simple and required plenty of muscle. The poorest farmers had only hoes and digging sticks. Most others had slightly more sophisticated implements such as axes, hooks, mallets, and shovels. Ploughs were used if the soil was not too rocky. Typical crops included corn, beans, and squash. If the farmer had livestock, he might grow hay to feed the animals. Tossing the hay required a pitchfork, often made from a sapling split at the end and splayed out.

Life on a farm could also be dangerous, as Ebenezer found out one day (and wrote about many years later, when he was seventy-five). "I left my work, being alone, to try my skill at riding on horseback; and, while attempting to put on the bridle, the horse suddenly bit a piece of flesh from my cheek, the scar of which is evident to this day."

In fact, Ebenezer enjoyed very little about Pelham's farm. "I imagined," he wrote, "that I suffered many privations and endured much hardship. Boys are apt to complain of their lot, especially when deprived of the indulgences of home."

As rumblings of revolt grew louder throughout the colonies, Ebenezer grew more resentful than ever. "A spirit of disaffection pervaded the land; groans and complaints, and injustice and wrongs were heard on all sides," he recalled. "I had for some time been dissatisfied with my situation, and was desirous of some change. I had made frequent complaints of a grievous nature to my father; but he paid no attention to them."

By the time Ebenezer was twelve years old, he and his friends (boys in situations similar to his own) had concluded that they were oppressed. "I thought that I was doing myself great injustice by remaining in bondage when I ought to go free," he wrote. "And that the time was come, when I should liberate myself from the thralldom of others, and set up a government of my own; or, in other words, do what was right in the sight of my own eyes."

Although Ebenezer was determined to gain his liberty, he did not want to undertake such a project alone. He approached a friend, an older boy named John Kelley, and pointed out that they both were "living in a state of servitude that ought to be scorned by the sons of freemen."

John agreed, and he and Ebenezer decided that they were capable of living on their own. They bundled up their belongings and hid the bundles in a barn some distance from where they lived. Then, at eight o'clock on the evening of April 18, 1775, they met on the church steps. By nine o'clock they were on their way to Providence, Rhode Island, where they hoped to become sailors.

When Ebenezer and John arrived in Dedham, Massachusetts, later that night, they noticed crowds gathering in the street. The boys exchanged worried glances. "Our fears induced us to think that the uncommon commotion . . . must have some connection with our escape," Ebenezer recalled. "And that the moving multitudes were in pursuit of us."

The boys tried to stay out of sight and, to their relief, no one seemed to recognize them. They headed for Walpole, planning to stop there for the night. At eleven o'clock they realized they were too tired to go that far and, using their bundles as pillows, they stretched out on the cold ground. The next morning they arrived in Walpole, where they stopped for a breakfast of bread and milk at a local tavern. To their delight, the landlord refused to accept any payment from them, probably because they seemed so young.

The level of anxiety in Walpole was much like that in Dedham. "People . . . frequently interrogated us respecting whence we came and whither we were going."

Fearful of being discovered and forced back into "slavery," Ebenezer and John gave only terse answers to questions. A tavern keeper asked, "Where are you going?" They replied, "To seek our fortunes." He responded, "You have taken hard times for it."

The boys soon found out what he meant. Earlier that morning a group of Americans had fought British troops at Lexington and

Concord, about 30 miles north of Walpole. The news of an American victory was greeted with "loud shouts of exultation," according to Ebenezer, "while the militia marched off full of ardor and zeal!"

Now Ebenezer and John knew what all the excitement had been about back in Dedham. Reassured that they were not being hunted, they turned their attention to satisfying their hunger and thirst. However, as Ebenezer put it, "Our funds would not permit us to indulge our appetites with the luxury of a dinner."

They were also tired of walking. Unable to afford the price of hiring a coach, they haggled energetically with a coachman to reduce the fare. The man finally agreed but insisted that one of the boys ride next to him and the other ride on the baggage. Writing years later in the 1830s, Ebenezer commented: "The coachman's seat on stagecoaches in those days was not the comfortable place which it now is; and . . . to sit upon the baggage could not be considered a great privilege. . . . It required not a little exertion to keep one's position."

Soon after arriving in Providence, the twelve-year-old and his companion took full stock of their situation. They were alone at sunset in a strange city and could only watch as people headed home after work to enjoy the company of family and friends.

"Solitary and desolate . . . we wandered about the streets," Ebenezer recalled. A meal at the local tavern was out of the question—too expensive. Plopping down on the steps of a church, they rummaged through their bundles, pulling out a few scraps of food. That night they slept in an empty cabin on a ship in the harbor.

The next morning they strolled through town, still feeling depressed. The time had come, they decided, to seek employment. Only later did Ebenezer realize that he and John had parted without making any arrangements to meet again. "After that day I never saw him," Ebenezer wrote. "I have since ascertained that [he] . . . went to sea. What was his fate I know not."

As Ebenezer wandered through town that day in 1775, he happened to stop at a markethouse. There, he encountered a man who seemed familiar to him. He was dressed in the typical fashion of the day: a wig and three-cornered hat as well as "a long coat of ample dimensions that appeared to have been made with reference to future growth; breeches with large buckles, and shoes fastened in the same manner."

The man's name was Obadiah Curtis, and he had recently come to Providence from Boston. He looked familiar because Ebenezer's aunt had worked for him in Boston. Ebenezer soon discovered that his aunt had moved to Providence with the Curtis family, and so he followed Mr. Curtis home.

Naturally, Ebenezer's aunt wondered what he was doing so far from home. The boy had to think fast. "I had to exercise not a little art, and to depart not a little from the truth to account for my unexpected visit," he wrote. His aunt managed to get the truth from him anyway and tried to convince him to give up the notion of going to sea. Her pleadings failed to persuade him, and she finally gave up trying. "To this good woman was I indebted for sustenance while I remained in Providence, and for many articles of clothing of which I was in great need," Ebenezer recalled.

Having insisted on his right to make his own way, Ebenezer set out to find a job. After a few days, he signed on as a cabin boy under Capt. Joseph Manchester. The ship was headed for Cape Francois on the island of Sainte Domingue. Ebenezer would earn twenty-one shillings per month, half of what the adult sailors were paid.

The boy from Roxbury hadn't been to sea before. The seasoned sailors called him a "green hand," a reference to his inexperience. The term could have also described his actual color during his bout of seasickness on the first few days of the cruise, but he grew used to the motion of the ship and regained his health and spirits. Although only twelve years old, he was eager to show the sailors that he was a valuable member of the crew. His efforts did not always achieve the desired result.

"Among other misfortunes," he later wrote, "I unluckily placed a large pot of butter in the larboard locker, without the precaution to fasten it in its place. It rolled out in the course of the night, and the fragments of the pot together with the contents were scattered about near the foot of the cabin steps."

At about this time, the captain chose to go below deck. He stepped into the greasy mixture, slipped, slid, and sprawled facedown in the butter.

"The butter received a stamp of considerable magnitude in the form of a head," Ebenezer recalled. "Which, although it served to protect the captain's from any lamentable damage, did not shield mine from a volley of oaths and threats arising from the irritation of the moment and the awkward predicament in which he found himself placed."

After arriving at Cape Francois about two weeks later, Ebenezer and the rest of the crew built barrels to hold the molasses they would be taking with them. They created the casks out of hoops and staves, or boards, using a technique called coopering.

By the time the ship returned to America, British ships were cruising the coastal waters. Ebenezer's vessel attempted to reach Providence without being discovered by the enemy. "If the breeze had continued favorable," he wrote, "we should have effected our object; but unfortunately, the wind subsided a little before daylight, and in the morning we found ourselves close by the enemy." Unable to escape, the crew ran the vessel ashore. The captain gave permission to all to get away as best they could. Concerned that Ebenezer would not be able to swim to shore, he advised the boy to stay on board and be taken prisoner.

"I hesitated a short time about taking his advice," Ebenezer recalled, "but finally concluded to run the risk of being drowned; and with nothing on but a shirt and a pair of trousers, I plunged into the sea and swam for the shore." Bullets whistled over his head. Fighting fatigue and fear, he battled the waves and finally made it to land. "In dread of pursuit, I ran into a cornfield," he wrote, "and finding my wet clothes an incumberance, I stripped them off and ran with all speed through the field." Soon he came upon the rest of his crew, who had escaped ahead of him. They found his condition most amusing.

"Holloa! My boy!" Ebenezer recalled one of them saying. "You cut a pretty figure; not from the garden of Eden, I can swear for it, for you have not even an apron of fig-leaves to cover you with: you were not born to be drowned, I see, though you may live to be hanged."

Another sailor took off one of two shirts he had on. The garment covered Ebenezer from shoulders to feet. Thus gowned, he fell in with the men, and before long they came to a house. The woman who lived there took pity on his "grotesque and unique condition" and gave him a decent suit of clothes.

Back in Providence, Ebenezer called again on his aunt. She was glad to see him but lectured him on the folly of his ways. When Ebenezer told her he intended to sign on for another voyage, she was shocked. In spite of her disappointment, she once again outfitted him for the journey.

Ebenezer's second cruise to Sainte Domingue was uneventful. After collecting his payment, he decided to go along with his aunt's wishes and return home. He felt a bit guilty about the worries he must have caused his parents, with the country in such an uproar.

He arrived in Roxbury in November 1775, six months older and wiser in the ways of the world. To his dismay, he learned that his parents had moved to Dorchester, about 3 miles away. That night he slept in the American barracks in Roxbury.

When he reached his parents' house in Dorchester, he was greeted by his mother, who was amazed to see him. She had given up hope. With a shriek of joy, she called to her husband, who was sick in bed with a cold. According to Ebenezer, Richard Fox was pleased that he had returned but not as excited as his wife. During Ebenezer's long absence, his father had continuously reassured her that their son would "no doubt be taken care of."

Writing years later in the 1830s, Ebenezer acknowledged, "It may appear surprising . . . that my aunt at Providence had not informed my parents respecting my movements. To say nothing of the fact, that she did not possess the pen of a ready writer, there were no regular means for conveying information in those days. Mails and post-offices, now so common, were then unknown. Situated as my aunt was, she could have but little access to travelers, and, being very domestic in her habits, she was seldom out of the house of her employer."

Once his initial pleasure at Ebenezer's survival wore off a bit, Richard Fox addressed him solemnly. "My son, I am much surprised and grieved that you should have left home in the manner you did. If you had any cause for complaint . . . why did you not inform me?"

Ebenezer was still smarting from the wrongs he felt he had suffered on the farm. He countered that he had complained, but no one had paid any attention to him.

"Even so," his father replied. "I hope you will abandon all such schemes in future. You can remain at home until you are old enough to learn a trade, and then choose one for yourself."

That winter, Ebenezer attended school and made himself useful around the house. He enjoyed visiting the American camp nearby and talking to the soldiers. In his memoirs he included a song he had heard that reminded him of his own experience.

Father and I went down to camp,
Along with Captain Gooding,
And there we see'd the men and boys
As thick as hasty-pudding.
Yankee Doodle, keep it up!
Yankee Doodle dandy;
Mind the music and the step,
And with the girls be handy.

The song, titled "Yankee Doodle Dandy," had been written by a British officer to make fun of the Americans. The "Yankees" adopted the tune as their own and played it proudly on fife and drum throughout the Revolution.

After Ebenezer turned thirteen, he and his brother James, who was fifteen, decided it was time to learn a trade and relieve their father of some of his burden. The British had evacuated Boston in March 1776, so Ebenezer and James went into town to seek jobs.

"I found employment in the shop of Mr. John Bosson, a barber and manufacturer of wigs," Ebenezer wrote later.

Wigs were big business in colonial America. Worn in England beginning in the 1660s, they had originally been highly curled and shoulder length. They grew larger and longer between 1680 and 1700, then shorter and smaller in the early 1700s. By the time Ebenezer entered his apprenticeship, wigs were made of straight hair that was pulled back into a short ponytail. Sometimes men purchased only the tail and attached it to their own hair. Before putting on a wig, men dressed it with a mixture of fat, cinnamon, and cloves, and powdered it with perfumed flour. In the homes of the wealthy, a powder room was provided for this purpose.

Ebenezer's main job was to prepare hair for wigs and other uses. The hair might be from a human, yak, goat, or horse. Shaving customers was usually Mr. Bosson's job, but occasionally Ebenezer was, in his words, "allowed to scrape the face of some transient customer, who might be reasonably expected never to call again for a repetition of the operation."

By the time Ebenezer was sixteen, the war against Britain was in full force. Bosson was called into service in the militia and was angry about this turn of events. At one point he glared at Ebenezer and another apprentice and said, "If either of you had the spunk of a louse, you would offer to go for me."

It was not unusual at the time for men to hire substitutes for military service if they could afford it. Ebenezer could not stop thinking about Bosson's words, especially since his family could certainly use the money. Finally, he offered to join the service in Bosson's place.

Although Ebenezer remained in the militia for a time, he soon felt the call of the sea. This time he sailed aboard the *Protector*, the largest ship in the Massachusetts navy.

In 1781 the ship was captured and Ebenezer was imprisoned on the *Jersey* prison ship. In order to escape the horrors of that place, he enlisted in the British army to serve in the West Indies.

After the war, at age twenty-one, he returned to work for Mr. Bosson as a barber, and for a time he served as postmaster of Roxbury. He later established his own business, selling "crockery, glass, and hard ware." Ebenezer Fox married Anna Downes of Connecticut. Based on census records, the couple had at least three children: Abraham Seaver, born in 1786, Ebenezer Downs, born in 1788, and Charles, born in 1794.

Ebenezer wrote his memoirs to amuse his grandchildren. One Thanksgiving, he had a bad cough and could not tell them the stories they loved to hear. Instead, he wrote several pages each day for one of the older grandchildren to read aloud to the others. His memoirs were published in 1838, five years before his death in December 1843.

TROUBLESOME TIMES

James Potter Collins

1763–1844

"These are the times that try men's souls," political essayist Thomas Paine wrote in December 1776. He spoke for multitudes. The year 1776 was one of great upheaval, tragedy, and sacrifice in the newly formed United States of America. More than a thousand American soldiers were killed or wounded in battle in Massachusetts, New York, and New Jersey. Patriots chased the enemy out of Boston that spring but lost New York City in the fall. By December, supplies were depleted. The soldiers of the Continental army were exhausted.

Even so, there were Americans whose souls had not yet been "tried" by the times. Down on the border between North and South Carolina, thirteen-year-old James Potter Collins wasn't giving the Revolution much thought. To be sure, a few skirmishes had rattled the South, and in June the British had attempted to invade Charleston, South Carolina, the largest city in the southern states. However, these events had not disrupted James's life. To him, Paine's "trying times" might as well have occurred in a foreign country.

James Collins was a tailor's apprentice. His employer—or master—provided him with food, clothing, and a place to live while he learned the tailoring trade, and James had no complaints. Years later, in his memoirs, he wrote that his master "was a man of very agreeable disposition, and remarkably good-humored, a good workman . . . so that I found myself placed in quite an agreeable situation."

The young apprentice began by learning simple tasks such as sewing lining. His job may have been agreeable, but it was also dull. As Christmas 1776 approached, James found himself with extra time on his hands. The tailor and his wife attended many holiday parties, leaving the thirteen-year-old to watch the house, and he quickly grew bored. One afternoon, the sight of the tailor's cat lounging before the fire gave him an idea.

He gathered some scraps of cloth from the shop and set to work. By evening, he had made a small suit of clothing, complete with coat and vest. Now all he had to do was get his "model" to cooperate.

"I caught the cat," he wrote. "Put on the whole suit . . . buttoned all on tight."

The cat was not amused. After trying in vain to get rid of the outfit, it escaped through a hole in the floor. Soon the tailor and his wife returned from their party. Filled with good humor, they and their friends began to pass around a bottle of rum.

"After all were seated around the fire," James wrote later, "who should appear but the cat in his uniform."

The tailor grabbed the cat. "Is this your day's work?" he asked James.

Thoroughly embarrassed, James admitted that it was. "To complete my mortification the clothes were carefully taken off the cat," he recalled, "and hung up in the shop for the inspection of all customers that came in."

James's father, Daniel Collins, was probably even less pleased than the cat with his son's antics. According to James, his father, a teacher, was "rigid in his discipline, both at school and at home." James wrote, "Every rule that he laid down, must be strictly complied with, or on failure, punishment was the inevitable consequence."

James was the fourth child of Daniel and Elizabeth Heland

Collins. He was born in what is now York County, South Carolina, on November 22, 1763. Several years later, Elizabeth Collins died giving birth to her seventh child. The baby also died.

"My father was then left with six children, all young," James related. "Some of the neighboring women took three of my sisters, and my father retained his sons at home."

A year or so after the death of James's mother, Collins married a young widow with one child. Thirteen children were subsequently born to the couple.

James and his siblings attended school in the winter and worked on the family farm during the summer. Every Sunday evening, they memorized and recited Bible verses. His father permitted "no fishing, shooting, hunting, or visiting on that day, or trading or dealing of any kind whatever."

In 1775, when James reached his twelfth birthday, his father offered to send him to college. James's reading and math skills were "tolerable," as James put it, and his father thought he should study divinity. James disagreed. Collins decided to use the college fund for other purposes—after all, he had a wife and twenty children to support. He arranged for James to become a tailor's apprentice for a term of five years. With so many children to clothe, having a tailor in the family would be helpful.

Meanwhile, British and American forces continued to fight. The patriots were victorious in battles at Trenton and Princeton, New Jersey, and at Saratoga, New York. British troops took control of Philadelphia in the fall of 1777, then lost it in the summer of 1778. By then the French had entered the conflict on the side of the rebels.

The British had to take a long, hard look at their strategy. They decided to move the war into the South. One reason was that the southern colonies were more valuable to England financially than the northern colonies. Southern plantations provided cash crops such as tobacco and rice, which the British government insisted should be exported to British ports, where they were taxed.

In addition, the British had always believed the king had more support in the South than in the North. They pictured southern Loyalists coming forth in huge numbers to ensure a victory for the Crown. Finally, by hanging on to the southern colonies, England could maintain an economic hold on the northern colonies.

On December 29, 1778, the British captured Savannah, Georgia. A month later they controlled the entire state. James's master decided to move further north into North Carolina. He sent James, now fourteen, back to his family.

Although the war was closer to home than before, James continued to live his life as usual. When he was not working, he was often up to mischief. He and one of his stepbrothers had a habit of sneaking into the cellar and filling half-pint gourds from their father's whiskey supply. "Our two gourds lasted us about three weeks or longer," James wrote later, "for we used it very sparingly."

At harvest time, while members of the community danced or talked around the fire, James and his friends conducted boxing matches "at a convenient distance from the house." Some of the older men approved of the fights, but Daniel Collins did not. No matter how sore James was after a match, he never complained once he got home. "If ever [my father] found out that I was in the boxing party," he explained, "I was sure to get a dressing which hurt worse than all the boxing I ever was in."

After a brief stint in college, James returned home and became a shoemaker's apprentice. He disliked the work, and after a time his father decided to apprentice James to a weaver instead. In colonial days, families made their own clothing, with men traditionally taking on the weaving and women the spinning.

Meanwhile, British activity in the Carolinas intensified. In March 1780, troops under British general Henry Clinton took another run at Charleston. When the city surrendered on May 12, James's neighbors along the North and South Carolina border took notice.

"Times began to be troublesome," James wrote, "and people began to divide into parties. Those that had been good friends . . . became enemies; they began to watch each other with jealous eyes, and were designated by the names of Whig and Tory. Recruiting officers were out in all directions, to enlist soldiers."

Prior to 1763, Whigs (liberals) and Tories (conservatives) had existed only in British politics. In America, people who supported the king's authority were called "Tories" by the Whigs, who were in favor of American independence.

American Whigs also had their own definition of Tory, as reported in the *New York Journal* in February 1775. "A tory is a thing with a head in England, a body in America, and a neck that needs stretching," they said, making a not-so-subtle reference to hanging. They were only half joking.

Soon the war that had once seemed so far away became personal for the Collins family. John Moffett, a captain in the South Carolina Militia, asked Daniel Collins if he would allow his son to become a "collector of news" for the militia. People were used to seeing sixteen-year-old James out and about, running errands for his father and others. He was therefore unlikely to arouse suspicion. Besides, as James put it, he knew "all the by-paths for twenty or thirty miles around."

"In order to prepare me for business, I had to receive several lectures," James wrote. "I was to attend all public places . . . and pay strict attention to all that was passing in conversation and otherwise."

James turned out to be good at the job. "Tories were several times disappointed in their plans without being able to account for the cause," he recorded later.

Unfortunately for James, the Tories learned about his spying activities and swore revenge. His father urged him to give up espionage, and James complied without protest. Daniel Collins had served in other wars, and he told James that being a member of the militia would be safer than acting as a spy. Sitting on the sidelines was not an option, according to Collins. "My son you may prepare for the worst," he told James. "The thing is fairly at issue. We must submit and become slaves, or fight."

James and his father joined Captain Moffett's band, a group who boasted the ability to be "mounted and ready at a minute's warning." They called themselves minutemen. As volunteers, the members expected no pay, and they furnished their own clothes, horses, saddles, and weapons. As was common in colonial times, they made their own bullets by melting lead. If lead was not available, they asked local citizens to donate old pewter dishes and spoons.

"Swords, at first, were scarce," James wrote. "But we had several good blacksmiths among us. If we got hold of a piece of good steel, we would keep it; and likewise, go to all the sawmills, and take all the old whip saws we could find . . . In this way we soon had a pretty good supply of swords and butcher knives."

Americans faced one defeat after another during the spring of 1780. Not only was Charleston captured but patriot forces were beaten at Monck's Corner and Lenud's Ferry, South Carolina, by troops under the command of British lieutenant colonel Banastre Tarleton.

On May 29 at Waxhaw Creek, Tarleton again defeated the rebels. The story quickly spread that the British officer had ordered his men (Americans serving in the British Legion) to slash to death more than one hundred patriots who were trying to surrender after the battle ended. The report was probably exaggerated, but from then on, the patriots referred to Tarleton as "The Butcher" or "Bloody Ban."

In mid-June, James traveled with John Moffett's militia to Ramsour's Mill in Lincoln County, North Carolina, to take part in a confrontation between Loyalists and patriots. But by the time the minutemen arrived, the battle was over. "After assisting some of the wounded and helping to bury the dead belonging to our own side, we retreated to our own place," James later recorded.

In July, Loyalist forces under Capt. Christian Huck burned an ironworks owned by patriot William "Billy" Hill, then set fire to Hill's home. Continuing on, Huck burned the homes of several other known rebels in York County.

Moffett and other patriot forces were determined to avenge the attacks. At daybreak on July 12, they crept up on Huck's camp at a plantation owned by James Williamson. Huck's sentinels spotted them, however, and fired their guns. There James got his first look at a troop of British cavalry. "They differed vastly in appearance from us poor hunting-shirt fellows," he noted.

Once the fighting began, James had no time to study the enemy's appearance. Rifle balls whistled and swords clanked. Huck was killed in the battle, and his men retreated.

"For my own part," James reported, "I fired my old shot gun only twice in the action. I suppose I did no more harm than burning so much powder."

Still, the times had not yet begun to "try" James Collins's soul, but that was about to change.

During the summer of 1780, several patriot victories helped build American confidence in the South. Guerilla fighter Francis Marion, the "Swamp Fox," reinforced the Continental army's efforts. Although the patriots suffered a devastating loss at Camden, South Carolina, in August, the momentum of the campaign was in their favor.

On August 18, Moffett's band headed south to lend their support to Brig. Gen. Thomas Sumter.

"We met Sumpter [sic] retreating rapidly," James recalled later. "We joined in the retreat until we came to Fishing Creek, a place where it was thought we could halt in safety, and rest."

Sumter's troops were on the run from none other than "Bloody Ban." The men were exhausted and hungry. After posting a guard, some kindled fires and began cooking, and others collapsed on the ground to sleep.

"All at once the picket guns gave the alarm," James wrote. "Before Sumpter could wake up his men and form, the enemy were among them cutting down everything in their way."

James and many of his comrades dashed across the creek and into the highlands. The shooting stopped and little by little, members of the militia straggled up the hill to join them. In James's words: "It was a perfect rout, and an indiscriminate slaughter."

As darkness descended, the men lay down to rest, their swords and guns close at hand. As it turned out, the British had killed and wounded 150 rebels, and more than 300 had been captured, including all the Continentals.

"After I had laid down," James later recalled. "I began to reflect. Well, thought I, if this be the fate of war, I would willingly be excused." However, he conceded, "The thing had gone too far, and there was no safety in retreating."

Returning to the battlefield the next morning, James again regretted his involvement. "The dead and wounded lay scattered in every direction over the field; numbers lay stretched cold and lifeless; some were yet struggling in the agonies of death, while here and there, lay others, faint with the loss of blood, almost famished for water, and begging for assistance."

Five members of Moffett's band were missing. Two were quickly found, "both setting up, unable to walk without assistance, and mangled by the sword." James never learned the fate of the other three. Guns and horses were among the spoils of the battle, and James acquired "a good looking rifle, with a shot-bag and all the apparatus belonging."

He put the gun to good use one rainy Saturday in October—at King's Mountain on the border of North and South Carolina. There, Moffett's minutemen joined more than 1,000 back-country patriots from Georgia, Virginia, and the Carolinas. Their goal was to bring down Maj. Patrick Ferguson and his Tory troops, who had stationed themselves upon a ridge. By the end of the day on October 7, 1780, Ferguson was dead, 400 Tories had been wounded or killed, and 700 had been taken prisoner. The patriots had suffered only eighty-eight casualties.

The sight of the vanquished enemy did not bring James joy. "I could not help turning away from the scene before me, with horror," he wrote. "And . . . could not refrain from shedding tears." The next morning, which was Sunday, he watched with genuine sorrow as "the wives and children of the poor Tories came . . . in great numbers."

Loyalists and patriots continued to clash on various South

Carolina battlegrounds: Tearcoat Swamp, Fish Dam Ford, Blackstocks, Long Cane, Halfway Swamp, and Hammond's Store. On a bitter-cold morning in January, James found himself at a meadow called the Cowpens—face-to-face with "Bloody Ban" Tarleton's British Legion.

"About sunrise on the 17th January, 1781, the enemy came in full view," James recalled. "The sight, to me at least, seemed somewhat imposing; they halted for a short time, and then advanced rapidly, as if certain of victory."

James was part of an army under the command of Daniel Morgan—an army consisting of militia from six states as well as a core group of Continental regulars and state troops. In total, they numbered between 800 and 1,000. Yet no one would have blamed James for being terrified. Morgan had placed him and about 300 other militiamen on the front line, directly in the path of the Loyalist cavalry.

"Give 'em two shots," Morgan had instructed the militia. "Just two shots. Then you can move off to the left. . . . Get around behind the hill, where you can straighten yourselves out."

Bayonets gleaming, the enemy charged. James fired two shots, then turned and dashed to his left. The enemy thundered after him. "Now my hide is in the loft," James thought as he ran for his life.

Fortunately, Morgan's strategy worked as planned. Intent on wiping out the militiamen, the astonished Loyalists discovered themselves suddenly surrounded by Morgan's cavalry. "The shock was so sudden and violent, they could not stand it, and immediately betook themselves to flight," James reported. "They appeared to be as hard to stop as a drove of wild Choctaw steers, going to a Pennsylvania market."

"Form, form, my brave fellows!" cried Morgan, waving his sword. "Give them one more fire and the day is ours."

Indeed it was. Tarleton's horse was shot from under him. He mounted another animal and attempted, without success, to rally his troops. In the end, he galloped away at top speed with a number of his men.

Although Tarleton escaped, more than one hundred of his soldiers had been killed in the one-hour battle, including ten officers. More than 700 Loyalists had been taken prisoner, 200 of them wounded. In all, Tarleton had lost nearly 90 percent of his force. The Battle of the Cowpens eventually became known as the turning point of the Revolution. The victory improved patriot morale, and the British began to realize they had overestimated Loyalist support in the South.

Throughout the rest of the war, James Potter Collins served as a scout and messenger. Afterward, at age twenty, he went "out into the world" to make his own way. At various times he worked as a teacher, a tailor, and a horse trader. He also was involved in the surveying and settling of the state of Georgia, and in peacekeeping efforts between pioneers and the Cherokee and Creek Indian tribes.

In 1793 James married Jane McNeil. She died childless in 1801. He married Mary Anderson in 1803, and together they had three children.

James wrote his memoirs in 1836 at age 73, while living in Louisiana. He died in Texas eight years later and was buried on the Collins farm north of Clarksville, near the Red River.

SO TIRED, SO SAD, AND SO SCARED

Frances Slocum

1773–1847

I first remember living far away in the east," the old woman told her nephew. "And our home was near the great sea water."

Ma-con-a-quah, as the woman was called, paused to let her son-in-law translate from the Miami language to English. She closed her eyes, trying to recall the earliest years of her life, a long time ago, when she was a little red-headed girl named Frances Slocum.

"We lived in a large house," she said. "My father was a Quaker and wore a broad-brimmed hat. He worked hard. My mother was a large woman and worked hard too."

The house Frances remembered was in Warwick, Rhode Island. Her parents were members of the religious Society of Friends (Quakers). Like most Quaker men, her father, Jonathan, wore a dark-colored hat with a low crown and broad brim. By the time Frances was born, he and his wife, Ruth Tripp Slocum, already had six children. Not surprisingly, both parents "worked hard."

In 1777, when Frances was four years old, her family headed west. "One day they brought a great, big wagon to our home," she recalled later. "It had a big tent over it. They filled it with many things from our home and then they put us children in. Father

Courtesy of the Tippecanoe County Historical Association

Frances Slocum

drove the wagon. Mother would sit by him part of the time and then she would be with us."

The children inside the wagon included Judith, who was nearly 17; William, age 15; Ebenezer, 11; Mary, 8; Benjamin, 6; Frances, 4; Isaac, 2; and Joseph, 1. Isaac Tripp, Frances's grandfather, traveled with them. Her eighteen-year-old brother, Giles, rode alongside on horseback, herding the cattle. "[Giles] would call me 'red head' and tell me that I should keep my head in or it would get bumped against the trees. We would get out of the wagon to eat and when evening came we would have some time to play before we went to bed."

Frances was probably too young to understand why her family was leaving Rhode Island. She had been only three in 1776, when America's thirteen colonies announced they would no longer remain under Great Britain's rule. Rhode Island's representatives, Stephen Hopkins and William Ellergy, had placed their signatures next to those of their countrymen on the official Declaration of Independence.

England and America were at war, but as Quakers, the Slocums were opposed to military action. Jonathan Slocum thought it best to remove his family from the coastal area, where most of the battles were taking place. Ruth Slocum knew it could be dangerous to remain in Rhode Island, but she wondered how safe frontier life would be. According to Frances, her mother was "afraid to go for she had heard about the Indians."

Ruth Slocum's concerns were not unfounded. Many people who traveled into "Indian country" brought back terrifying stories of Native American attacks on settlers. Some did not even live to tell their stories. The long trip west gave Ruth plenty of time to imagine the best and the worst of what might lie ahead. She had no way of knowing that in less than a year her darkest fears would be realized.

"We spent many days going from the great sea water to the large river near where we made our new home," Frances told her nephew George Slocum years later.

The Slocums' new home was in the Wyoming Valley in western Pennsylvania. Located on the Susquehanna River and cradled by two mountain ranges, the valley offered fertile farmland as well as plenty of customers for Jonathan Slocum's blacksmith shop. The Slocums moved into a two-story log house on the edge of the woods near Wilkes-Barre Fort.

The Wyoming Valley may have appeared peaceful, but it had a troubled history. Count Zinzendorf, a Moravian missionary who arrived in 1742, had been on good terms with local Native Americans. However, his work was interrupted when the Delaware and Shawnee tribes declared war on each other. In 1762 about 200 colonists built the first settlement. Iroquois warriors murdered a Delaware chief and blamed the deed on the Europeans. In retaliation, the Delawares attacked the settlement in the spring of 1763, killing many of the inhabitants, including women and children.

Undaunted by the reports of violence, colonists continued to arrive. By the time the Slocums appeared on the scene in 1777, a cycle of attack and revenge was firmly established between Europeans and Native Americans in the region. The colonists relied on several forts along the Susquehanna River for protection, although these were little more than fortified houses. The Slocums' new home was half a mile from the nearest fort.

When the American Revolution first broke out, colonial and British leaders encouraged native tribes to remain neutral, to stay out of what amounted to a "family squabble." Before long, though, both sides began to court Native Americans, offering promises of a prosperous future, not to mention rewards for enemy scalps.

Whereas Britain had a history of trying to protect native lands, the colonists continually invaded those lands. The British paid good prices for trade items such as furs, and they always came "bearing gifts." The newly formed colonial government did neither. Many Native Americans could see no reason to support the "Big Knives," as they called the rebels. Others were lured by the possibility that a fourteenth state might be established for them after the war, complete with representation in the American Congress.

These developments increased tensions in the valley, but Jonathan Slocum still believed his family was safe. He was kind to Native Americans and they knew he was a Quaker—opposed to war and killing. As Frances put it: "My mother was afraid but my father . . . said the Indians were friends to the Quakers and would not hurt us."

The Slocums focused on everyday survival. Frances's older brothers and sisters had many chores to do, including collecting wood, making fires, feeding animals, grating and pounding corn, and fetching water from the spring. They scrubbed and swept with split brooms made from small sapplings. On wash days, they carried clothes to and from the pond. Crops had to be planted and harvested, and cows had to be milked and sheep sheared. Meals had to be cooked and served. Although Frances was young, she was expected to do her part.

"[My mother] would have all of us work," she later told her nephew George.

Like most children, Frances and her siblings experienced their share of injuries. A cart rolled over Ebenezer's foot, leaving him lame. Joseph accidentally struck Frances's left hand with a hammer, disfiguring her forefinger. Still, they were all alive and well in the summer of 1778.

On July 3, everything changed. British colonel John Butler arrived in the Wyoming Valley with more than 1,000 Loyalist troops and Native American allies. Butler demanded that the colonists surrender the forts. When the demand was not met, Butler's forces attacked. "The Indians and the other white men came and killed many people near our home," Frances recalled, "and burned many homes not far away."

The men and boys of the Wyoming Valley militia fought back, but they were outnumbered three to one. When the encounter was over, more than 300 settlers were dead, including women and children who had gathered at a fort for protection. Many who survived the massacre fled into the forest, where some eventually died of starvation or exposure.

The August 3 edition of the *Boston Gazette and Country Journal* reported: "The enemy took away some of the unhappy prisoners, and shutting up the rest in the houses, set fire to them, and they were all consumed together. After burning all the buildings in the fort they proceeded to the destruction of every building and improvement (except what belonged to some Tories)."

Poet Thomas Campbell lamented the event in a poem titled "Gertrude of Wyoming":

> On Susquehanna's side, fair Wyoming!
> Although the wild-flower on thy ruin'd wall,
> And roofless homes, a sad remembrance bring,
> Of what thy gentle people did befall;
> Yet thou wert once the loveliest land of all . . .

The Slocum house was not attacked on July 3, and Jonathan Slocum may have taken this as a sign that his family would continue to be safe. What he did not know was that his nineteen-year-old son, Giles, had been part of the Wyoming Valley militia that challenged John Butler's troops.

"My brother helped his white friends fight the Indians," Frances recalled. "My father told him he should not do that, for the Indians would never forget it. They would hold it against him."

Following the July 3 attack, many of the settlers headed back east, but the Slocums remained. Ruth was expecting a baby and could not tolerate a long trip. Not only that, Jonathan was certain that supporting his wife and children would be much harder in Rhode Island than in the Wyoming Valley. Above all, he still could not imagine local Native Americans harming his loved ones.

In September 1778, the Slocums' tenth child, Jonathan, was born. The household grew even larger as the Slocums took in two boys, Nathan and Wareham Kingsley, of Connecticut, after their father was captured by Native Americans. Although straggling bands of Native Americans continued to raid the valley, Frances and her family remained safe. Unfortunately, their period of immunity was about to end.

On November 2, Frances's father and grandfather were at the fort about half a mile away. Her mother was in the house, and Nathan and Wareham were outside sharpening a knife. Nathan, the eldest, was wearing a soldier's coat to ward off the November chill.

Five-year-old Frances was playing outside when she heard a gun go off. She looked up and saw Nathan lying on the ground. Several men stood over him, their dark skin streaked with bright color. Frances thought they might belong to the tribe her parents called Delaware, but the Delaware had always been friendly to Quakers. These men did not look friendly. Nathan was bleeding. Frances watched as one man took out a knife and grabbed Nathan by the hair. Horrified, she ran for the house.

Ruth Slocum had heard the gunshot. As soon as she saw what was happening, she shouted to her children to run and hide. Years later Frances told her nephew, "My big sister took my little brother and ran towards the fort. I hid under the stairs. The Indians went through our house and took some things. Then they saw my feet and where I was hiding. They pulled me out and started to leave with me and my crippled brother."

As the Delawares turned to go, Frances's mother rushed out of her hiding place, baby Jonathan in her arms. She pointed out that Ebenezer was lame and would be of no use. Her words had the desired effect, but her relief was short-lived. "They left my crippled brother," Frances said, "but took me and [Wareham]. My mother cried. I cried."

Ruth Slocum begged the men to release her daughter, but they ignored her. One of them put Frances over his shoulder and headed for the woods. Sobbing, Frances stretched out one hand and called for her mother. With the other hand, she pushed her auburn curls away from her face. That sight burned in Ruth Slocum's memory for the rest of her life.

The tribe that kidnapped Frances Slocum was indeed the Delaware. They called themselves Lenni Lenape, meaning "original people" or "common people." English settlers who encountered them in the 1600s gave them the name "Delaware" because they lived along the Delaware River. Back then Delawares could be found not only in Delaware but also in New Jersey, eastern Pennsylvania, and southeastern New York.

By 1778 European diseases and wars with other tribes had dramatically reduced the Delaware population, and colonial expansion had forced them to relocate many times. At one point, the land they inhabited was literally sold out from under them by the Iroquois confederacy. The Iroquois considered the Delawares a conquered people, subject to Iroquois rule.

Like many tribes during the Revolutionary War, the Delaware had pro-British and pro-American factions. Although many of the Delawares backed the British, a Delaware leader named White Eyes pledged to support the Americans. It was White Eyes who insisted that the agreement with the colonists include a promise to "form a state whereof the Delaware nation shall be the head, and have a representative in Congress." He got his wish, but government negotiators made sure to add a disclaimer: Nothing would be considered final until Congress approved the agreement.

That approval never came.

Jonathan Slocum had made every effort to assure Native Americans in the Wyoming Valley that he was neutral. However, he knew that Delawares who supported the British might have recognized Giles during the battle on July 3. That would be reason enough for a raid. As he himself had told Frances: "The Indians . . . never forget."

Jonathan and his father-in-law, Isaac, rushed home as soon as they heard about the abduction. A search party failed to find the children or their captors.

"The Indians did not take us so far on that day," Frances recalled. "They came to a cave and there we stayed all night. . . . I was so tired and so sad and so scared."

She remembered catching a glimpse of her father from the cave. "I was going to scream," she said, "when an Indian held a big knife over me and looking cross, said, 'me kill, me kill.' That was the last time I saw my father."

The search party finally had to admit defeat. Jonathan did not want to give up, but it was extremely dangerous to venture into the wilderness.

In spite of their fears, the Slocums held out hope that they would find Frances soon and that the Delawares had satisfied their desire for revenge. Less than two months later, their hopes were dashed. Frances was still missing, and on December 16 the Delawares struck again.

Frances's father, grandfather, and brother William were feeding cattle when the shooting started. Jonathan fell to the ground, dead. Isaac was shot, then killed with a spear. Wounded in the heel, William managed to escape. He hobbled to the nearest fort to sound the alarm, but the attackers vanished into the woods before anyone could respond.

By then, Frances was far from home. Her initial terror had subsided considerably. The Delawares treated stolen children kindly. Several days after her capture, she had arrived at a large Delaware village at what is now Athens, Pennsylvania. There, the women had welcomed her with open arms.

"They seemed to like my red hair," Frances noted later. "The Indian women knew I was lonesome for my mother. So they held me as mother used to do. They made me pretty moccasins. . . . They made a little cup for me to drink out of."

Frances was taken north up the Susquehanna River, spending many nights in Delaware villages. After crossing under Niagara Falls, she arrived at a village larger than any she had seen before. Wareham had remained with her up until this point, but now he was taken away, and Frances never saw him again.

"But I was not so lonesome," she told her nephew years later. "For I was beginning to talk with Indian boys and girls. They tried to talk to me, and soon I began to understand what they were saying to me."

According to Delaware custom, Frances was given to a couple to replace a child who had died. Her adoptive parents were a Delaware chief named Tuck Horse and his wife.

"My hair was dressed in the Indian way," she recalled. "They painted my face and skin like the Indians. They put a wampum-bead dress on me. It was very pretty. All this with my moccasins made me look like an Indian. I thought I looked very fine."

That winter, Frances saw many Europeans in the Delaware village. "They were bringing the Indians guns and knives so they could go down and get more scalps," she said. "I never liked scalps, but the white men would do the same to the Indian if he could. Only the white men did not take scalps but he would kill squaws and papooses as well as braves. I often felt bad about the fighting, but what could I do? I did sometimes wonder whether they would get my father and brothers."

In the spring of 1779 Frances traveled with the tribe for many days through the woods and across lakes and rivers. "I thought it funny to sit in the canoe and put my hand in the water while the Indian rowed the boat," she said later.

The group finally set up camp near the Sandusky River in what is now Delaware County, Ohio. They stayed there for several months. As winter approached again, they made their way back to Niagara Falls.

The fighting continued. By this time, Spain and France had also declared war on Great Britain. Frances and her new family relocated on the Detroit River, where they stayed for about three years.

"I learned about the Great Spirit, Mon-da-min," Frances said years later. "The Indians told me about their God, Man-i-to. They told me also about the evil spirit, Mas-ko-na-ko. I remembered that my mother used to tell me something like that, only the names of the spirits were different."

On October 19, 1781, British general Charles Cornwallis formally surrendered to the American general George Washington at Yorktown, Virginia. The fighting on the frontier, however, was far from over. In the spring of 1782, Frances and the others in her village received terrible news: American militiamen had killed a group of Delawares in Ohio. The Native Americans, who had been converted to Christianity by Moravian missionaries, had refused to take sides in the conflict between Britain and America. In spite of this, the colonists blamed them for raids conducted by other tribes. On March 8 nearly one hundred Delaware men, women, and children were rounded up and told they were being taken to safety. Instead, they were murdered.

Frances's adoptive father, Tuck Horse, declared: "Indians must fight the white men, or they [will] drive us all out."

The preliminary articles of peace signed by Britain and America on November 30, 1782, did not mention Native Americans. Great Britain ceded to the United States all lands east of the Mississippi. None of the Native Americans living on those lands were included in negotiations. Once the Treaty of Paris was finalized in 1783, the United States government set about putting the treaty's terms into effect.

In their continuing search for Frances, Giles and William Slocum went to Niagara, where prisoners taken by Native Americans were being gathered for return to their families. Frances was not there. The brothers offered a reward for information about her and traveled throughout Ohio looking for her, but none of their efforts succeeded. Meanwhile, Wareham Kingsley was returned by his captors. All he could tell the anxious Slocums was that Frances had been treated well by the Delawares. He did not know where she was.

Frances grew up and eventually married She-po-ca-nah, a chief of the Miami tribe. She and her husband had two daughters and two sons, but the boys died. Frances was happy with her life. She did not seek out the Slocums because she was afraid they would try to take her away from people she had grown to love.

In 1807, Ruth Slocum passed away. Her children and grandchildren promised they would continue to search for Frances, and they did—for the next thirty years. Finally, in 1837, a woman was located who sounded like she could be Frances. The widow of a Miami chief, she lived near Peru, Indiana.

Frances's brother Isaac went to meet the woman, who was called Ma-con-a-quah, at her large double cabin in Deaf Man's Village. He wasn't sure she was his long-lost sister until he saw her left hand. The forefinger was disfigured, the nail missing.

"How came that finger injured?" he asked.

"My brother struck it with a hammer in the shop, a long time ago, before I was carried away," she replied.

Not long after her meeting with Isaac, Frances was reunited with her brother Joseph and sister Mary. She introduced them to her daughters. At first she was reserved, even distrustful, but she eventually grew comfortable enough to tell her siblings all that had happened to her. As time went on, she invited her nephew George Slocum and his wife, Eliza, to come and live near her.

"You shall be my son and share my best things," she told him. George accepted, and in 1846 he and Eliza moved into a cabin near Deaf Man's Village.

In March of 1847, Frances Slocum died at the age of seventy-four and was buried beside her husband and two sons.

WITH LIBERTY FOR ALL

James Forten

1766–1842

As the year 1773 drew to a close, tension mounted in Britain's thirteen American colonies. Colonial resistance to England's latest regulations and import taxes, or duties, threatened to boil into outright rebellion.

"Taxation without representation is tyranny!" declared lawyer James Otis.

His statement quickly became a battle cry for many Americans, but the words did not inspire James Fortune of Philadelphia. James knew almost nothing about taxation and even less about representation. He was just seven years old in 1773. His parents—free African Americans living in Philadelphia—would have appreciated Otis's viewpoint, but such matters did not concern James.

Born on September 2, 1766, James was the son of Thomas and Margaret Weymouth Fortune. (In later years, James would change his last name to Forten. Biographers suggest he did so because Fortune was a common slave name.) James had an older sister, Abigail, born in 1763.

His father's sister, Ann Elizabeth Fortune, also lived in Philadelphia. She was not only free but also fairly well-off financially. When she died in 1768, she named Abigail as her heir. The will stated that the child's inheritance would come to her at age twenty-one. Presumably James's aunt counted on James learning a trade

Courtesy of the Historical Society of Pennsylvania (HSP), Leon Gardiner Collection

James Forten

and earning a good living, whereas Abigail would need a decent dowry to attract a husband.

Thomas and Margaret Fortune rented a tiny wooden house in the Dock Ward section of town. Most of the houses in Philadelphia were small due to high building costs, and in many cases the large front room doubled as a place of business. Thomas Fortune, however, earned his living in a warehouse near the docks, where he worked as a sailmaker.

Young James would have gone to the sail loft with his father on many occasions. Boys were often put to work picking through scraps of canvas or cordage, sweeping the floor, and forming wax into blocks the size of a man's palm. Sailmakers ran their thread through these wax blocks before they started sewing. This made the stitching last longer because it resisted water.

In the 1700s, Philadelphia was known for its ships—brigs and schooners, topsail sloops, and ketches. Situated on the Delaware River, the city was a major port and shipbuilding center. One visitor called Philadelphia "happy, peaceful, elegant, hospitable, and polite." Others complained about the noise from carriages and wagons. As progressive as it was, Philadelphia still had traces of a rural atmosphere. In the summer, visitors remarked on the loud croaking of the bullfrogs who thrived in the ponds that dotted the city's edges.

In December 1773, angry human voices added to the noise level as thousands of Philadelphians gathered to protest the arrival of the British tea ship *Polly*. A group calling itself "The Committee for Tarring and Feathering" printed a handbill chastising the ship's captain. "Captain Ayres . . . ought to have known our People better," the notice read, "than to have expected we would be so mean as to suffer his rotten tea to be funnel'd down our Throats, with the Parliament's Duty mixed with it."

Seeing the protesting crowd, Captain Ayers opted to leave rather than be covered in tar and feathers. He turned the *Polly* around and went back to England. A little more than a week later, up in Boston, a group of Americans disguised as Indians boarded three English tea ships and dumped their cargo into the harbor.

For James Fortune, these dramatic incidents were overshadowed by an event of a much more personal nature. He would remember 1773 not because of tea or taxation, but because during the final weeks of that year, his father fell ill and died.

Records do not show the cause of Thomas Fortune's death, but disease was common and often fatal in colonial times. Philadelphia was a crowded city, giving rise to sanitation problems, and medical knowledge and expertise were limited.

Too young to earn his keep as an apprentice, James was sent to the African School, established by the Society of Friends (Quakers). There he learned how to read and do basic arithmetic, called "ciphering." His mother and sister took whatever work they could find, but making ends meet was difficult. At age nine, James left school and got a job with a local storekeeper. When he was not working, he liked to play marbles with his friends. He had a knack for the game and usually won.

Philadelphia became the meeting place for the Continental Congress. Delegates from the colonies got together to try to settle America's differences with Britain. However, on April 19, 1775, shots fired at Lexington and Concord ended those efforts. The following month the Second Continental Congress convened a few blocks from James Fortune's home. Among the notables in attendance were John Hancock, Benjamin Franklin, Thomas Jefferson, and John Adams.

As young James went about his work, he no doubt heard African-American men talking about what their role in the war might be. Those who were slaves had much to consider. The tide had already begun to turn against slavery in Philadelphia. Attacks on the slave trade appeared regularly in newspapers. Essayist Thomas Paine questioned how white Americans could "complain so loudly of attempts to enslave them" and still be slaveholders themselves.

In 1774 Philadelphia masters had begun to manumit, or release, large numbers of slaves. Even so, there were no guarantees—at least not from the colonists. A council of war headed by George Washington voted in October 1775 to reject the involvement of African Americans in military service. General orders from George Washington dated November 12 rejected blacks, boys too young to bear arms, and old men who were unfit to endure the hardships of war. It went without saying that women were excluded.

Also in November, Lord Dunmore, royal governor of Virginia, issued a proclamation. He promised freedom to all slaves and indentured servants who joined the king's forces. Soon Dunmore had formed the Black Regiment, which consisted of escaped Virginia slaves.

James probably heard many a spirited discussion about the options for blacks. Would a colonial victory lead to the liberation of slaves? Would it be better to enlist with the British and gain freedom immediately? Even free African Americans were not sure which side to choose.

On July 8, 1776, banker John Nixon read the Declaration of Independence aloud to a cheering throng at the State House in Philadelphia. The words sounded important to James, but he did not think all the talk of "unalienable rights" and being "absolved from allegiance to the British Crown" would have much of an effect on him.

Over the next few months, the British defeated the Continental army under Gen. George Washington at Long Island, Manhattan, and White Plains, New York. By December, the people of Philadelphia were on edge. They feared a British invasion but instead suffered a different sort of attack. Smallpox and camp fever erupted among the troops stationed in the city. Now, as James walked past the huge stone prison at Sixth and Walnut, he saw men digging long trenches that would eventually serve as graves for more than 2,000 people.

Upon viewing the sight, John Adams, Massachusetts delegate to the Continental Congress, wrote: "I never in my whole life was so affected with melancholy. . . . The graves of the soldiers . . . dead of smallpox and camp diseases, are enough to make the heart of stone [sic] to melt away."

In spite of these difficulties, Philadelphia was booming as 1776 drew to a close. New dwellings had gone up all over town. Early in the new year, however, residents noticed that prices were rising.

America's major supplier, Great Britain, was now the enemy. Philadelphians soon began to feel the impact of this fact on the availability and affordability of clothing, tools, and other necessities.

Writing during the winter of 1776–77, James Lovell, congressional delegate from Massachusetts, described the town as "a place of crucifying expenses." Judge Edward Shippen of Philadelphia commented, "The scarcity and advanced price of every necessary of life makes it extremely difficult for those who have large families."

In September 1777, James celebrated his eleventh birthday. He also experienced firsthand what Philadelphians had been dreading for months: the arrival of the British. Washington and his troops had been defeated at Brandywine. Anyone who had watched the American soldiers parade through Philadelphia a month earlier was not surprised. It was obvious they were struggling. They had no uniforms and no shoes. The all-white complexion of the Continental army had also changed. Washington needed every man he could get. Race was no longer an issue.

British and Hessian troops marched into Philadelphia on September 26. The Hessians were German soldiers hired by England. They were called Hessians because some of them, including several of their leaders, came from the German principality of Hesse.

King George III's men remained in Philadelphia until June 1778. By then France had entered the war on the side of the Americans. The British agreed to a prisoner exchange as well as the evacuation of Philadelphia. Soon the French ambassador arrived, and a grand banquet was held in his honor. In spite of food and clothing shortages among many, there seemed to be no shortage of parties. Wealthy women devoted themselves to acquiring the latest headdress. Judge Shippen wrote that he might have to move to another town in order to afford the lifestyle preferred by his "fashionable daughters."

General Washington decried the foolishness and extravagance of Philadelphia's ladies and gentlemen during his stay in the town from December 1778 to February 1779. Meanwhile, James and his family did the best they could in the face of severe inflation and shortages.

For the next four years, fighting in the South took center stage. Up north in Philadelphia, hardships continued. In May 1779, Philadelphia was the scene of food riots in which men with clubs attacked shopkeepers. The mob seized and jailed three merchants accused of deliberately charging higher prices than necessary.

The weather was also a challenge at times. James shivered through the winter of 1780, which later became known as "the hard winter." Ice on the Delaware River was nearly 20 inches thick, and frost was 5 feet deep in the ground.

Costs continued to climb. People hoarded scarce goods. The older James got, the more he worried about his mother and sister. One day as he walked along the river looking at the ships, he suddenly thought of a way to help his family and his country at the same time.

Unlike the slaves and free blacks who had fled Philadelphia with the British, James chose to support the American cause. In the words of a friend years later, "His heart was tried within him, on account of the wrongs his country was suffering from Great Britain."

In 1781, a few months before his fifteenth birthday, James enlisted as a powder boy on the *Royal Louis*, an American privateer. Privateers were ships owned by private individuals but armed and commissioned by the government to capture or destroy enemy ships. Cargo from these vanquished vessels was taken to American ports and sold, with the resulting "prize money" being shared by all crew members.

The *Royal Louis* was named for America's ally, King Louis XVI of France. The ship carried a crew of 200 men and 22 guns, or cannon. The ship's commander, Stephen Decatur, was a Rhode Islander whose father had been a French navy officer.

As a powder boy, it was James's job to stand behind the gun crew during battles and pass powder and cannonballs to the gunners. He was also expected to lend a hand anywhere else he was needed.

The ship set out on its first cruise in July 1781, and James quickly learned how to perform his duties. When he was not working, he sometimes challenged the other sailors to a game of marbles. They all admitted he was difficult to beat.

The *Royal Louis* had not been at sea very long before James experienced his first battle. He never forgot it. Years later, his son-in-law Robert Purvis described the scene he had heard James talk about many times: "He found himself amid the roar of cannon, the smoke of blood [sic], the dying and the dead." In the words of a family friend, "Every one was killed at the gun at which he was stationed, but himself."

After an extremely successful cruise with many prizes taken, the *Royal Louis* returned to port. Since he wasn't yet sixteen, James was given only one-half of a full share of the winnings, which was still far more than he could earn as a storekeeper. He gave most of his prize money to his mother and eagerly signed on for the next trip.

By then it was October 1781. On October 19, Lord Charles Cornwallis surrendered his troops to Washington at Yorktown. However, the war was not finished yet. About 30,000 British troops were still in North America, and all of America's major ports except Boston and Philadelphia were still under British control. At sea, the Revolution raged on.

Well into its second cruise, the *Royal Louis* gave chase to a ship. It could have been a merchant ship—easy pickings and a profitable day. Unfortunately for Decatur and his crew, the vessel they pursued was the *Amphion*, a British man-of-war. James and the other sailors prepared to fight. Suddenly, they saw two more ships looming on the horizon. They, too, were British.

The *Royal Louis* fled the scene but wasn't fast enough to outrun the *Amphion*. Recounting James's feelings as his ship surrendered and struck its sails, Robert Purvis said, "It was at this juncture that his mind was harassed with the most painful forebodings, from a knowledge of the fact that rarely, if ever, were prisoners of his complexion exchanged; they were sent to the West Indies, and there doomed to a life of slavery."

Once aboard the *Amphion*, James lined up with his crewmates to face inspection by Captain Bazely. To his surprise, Bazely took interest in the bag of marbles James carried. Bazely said his twelve-year-old son would enjoy a game.

The two boys got along so well that Bazely eventually offered to send James to England, where he would receive an education and live in comfort. Bazely was astonished when James did not leap at the chance but instead refused, explaining that he could not be a traitor to his country.

Disappointed, Bazely nevertheless thought well of the young patriot. Just before James was transferred to a prison ship, he gave him a note to show the commander. In it, Bazely praised James and recommended that he be exchanged at the first opportunity. In later years James liked to say that a game of marbles had saved him from a life of servitude in the West Indies.

James and his crewmates were imprisoned aboard the *Jersey*. Located in Wallabout Bay in the East River off Long Island, the black hulk was a sore sight for anyone's eyes. The *Jersey* floated ominously on the water, a cage of misery, pain, and death. Close up, the stench was unbearable.

Meals on the *Jersey* typically consisted of small amounts of meat, dried peas, and moldy, worm-infested biscuits. Exercise for the prisoners involved walking up and down the deck, shoulder to shoulder, in platoons. At sunset each evening, the men were packed together down below.

After being onboard only a short while, James found Daniel Brewton, age fourteen, who had also been on the *Royal Louis*. The conditions on the *Jersey* were especially hard on the younger boy, who soon grew pale, thin, and sickly.

James had been on the *Jersey* four months when he thought of a way to escape. An officer from the Continental navy was being exchanged for a British officer, and James asked if he could hide in the man's sea chest during the night and be carried ashore the next morning. The officer agreed but said he would deny any involvement if James were discovered.

Darkness fell and James prepared to execute his plan. At some point, however, he changed his mind. When the American naval officer stepped on shore the next morning, James was not in his trunk—Daniel Brewton was.

Realizing that the younger boy would die if he did not get off the *Jersey*, James had convinced Daniel to climb into the sea chest and had then helped the officer carry the chest off the ship. Daniel never forgot what James did for him. He confirmed the story often as an adult. When James died at home many years later, Daniel Brewton was by his side.

About three months after Daniel escaped, James was released in a general prisoner exchange. He walked more than 100 miles from Long Island to Philadelphia. Starting out barefoot, his clothing in rags, he eventually got help in Trenton, New Jersey, where kind citizens resupplied him. His reunion with his mother and sister was both joyful and shocking—they had been told he was dead.

In the years that followed, James worked as a sailmaker for Robert Bridges, the same man for whom his father had worked. When Bridges retired, he gave control of the business to James.

As an adult, James changed his last name to Forten. In 1803, he married Martha Beatte, who passed away about a year later, and in 1805 he married Charlotte Vandine. By then he had begun to take his place among Philadelphia's successful merchants. James and Charlotte had nine children: Margaretta, Charlotte, Harriet, James Jr., Sarah Louisa, Mary Isabella, Robert Bridges, Thomas Willing Francis, and William Deas.

Highly regarded as a businessman, philanthropist, and inventor, James perfected and patented a device that improved the method of raising sails. He was one of the first members of St. Thomas' African Episcopal Church and served on the Board of Trustees of a school established by the church in 1804. During the War of 1812, he enlisted 2,500 African Americans to help defend Philadelphia. He was awarded a certificate by the Humane Society in 1821 for rescuing people from drowning on four different occasions.

A staunch abolitionist, James Forten was a powerful voice for people of color during the 1800s. He actively opposed the efforts of the American Colonization Society, a group organized for the purpose of sending American blacks to live in a colony in Africa. Along with William Lloyd Garrison and others, James played a significant role in the formation of the American Anti-Slavery Society. In a speech to the Ladies' Anti-Slavery Society in 1836, he said: "I love America; it is my native land . . . I love the stars and stripes, emblems of our National Flag—and long to see the day when not a slave shall be found resting under its shadow."

In the meantime, James did what he could for those in bondage by serving on the Vigilant Committee of the Underground Railroad.

When James Forten died in 1842, the *Philadelphia Public Ledger* estimated that his funeral procession included "three to five thousand people, white and colored, male and female."

At the funeral, a young man James had befriended declared: "Every person was his neighbor, he recognized in all a brother, a child of the same common parent, an heir of immortality, and a fellow traveler to eternity."

Robert Purvis called James "a model, not as some flippant scribbler asserts, for what is called 'colored men,' but for all men."

James Forten was long gone by the time the United States abolished slavery. Yet he had played a role in liberating the people of his race, just as he had fought for the future of all Americans during the Revolution. In both cases, he did not hesitate to do battle for what he believed was right.

PREPARE TO HEAR AMAZING THINGS

Sally Wister

1761–1804

Sally Wister tried to stay calm as she packed her clothes in a large trunk. She and her parents, sisters, and baby brother were leaving their beautiful home in Philadelphia. Sally had no idea when they would return—or what they would find when they did.

It was not unusual for the Wisters to go away. They owned a country house in nearby Germantown, where Sally had spent many pleasant hours away from the disease and heat of Philadelphia. This time, however, they were not going to Germantown, nor were they traveling for enjoyment. They were leaving because their lives might be in danger if they stayed.

England's thirteen American colonies were, in the words of Britain's King George III, "in open and avowed rebellion." In April 1775 British troops had clashed with American militiamen at Lexington and Concord, Massachusetts. Since then, the British had won the Battle of Bunker Hill in Boston, and fighting had occurred in several other colonies, including South Carolina, New Jersey, and New York.

Sally's father, Daniel Wister, had followed the reports of military action. He was certain the British would try to capture Philadelphia. After all, Philadelphia was the meeting place of the

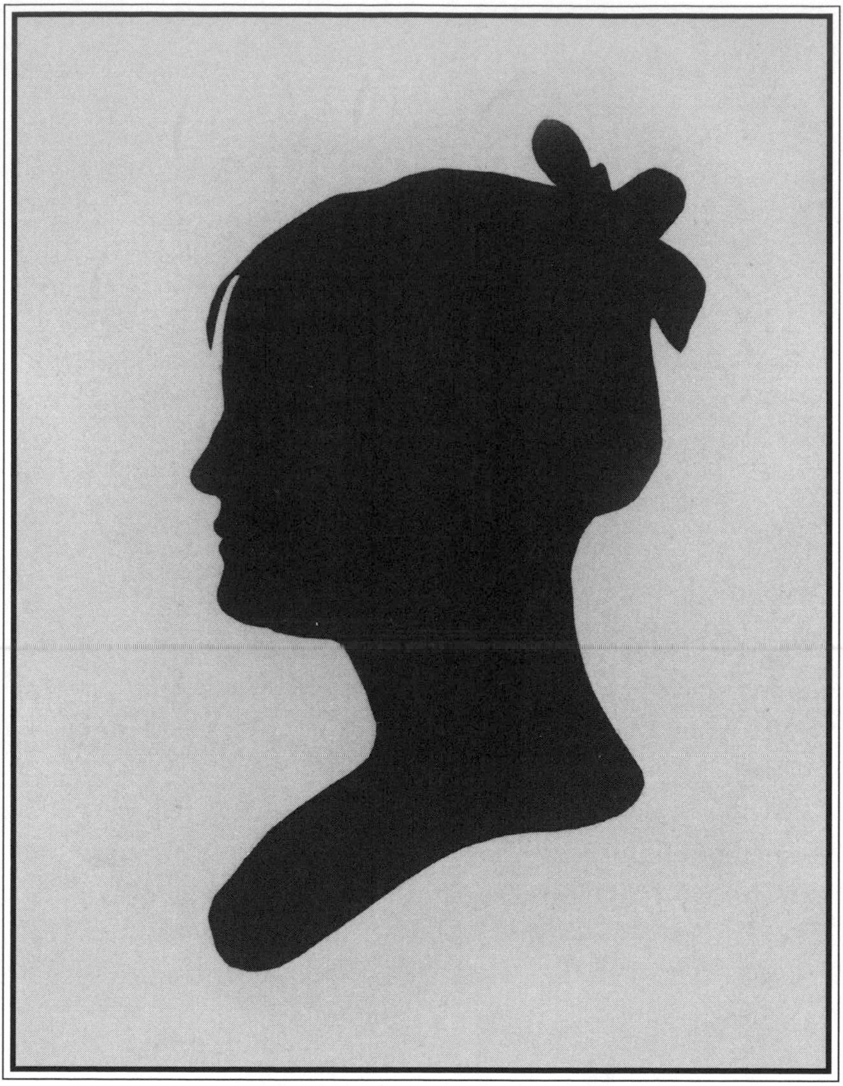

Silhouette of Sarah (Sally) Wister

Continental Congress and the city where the Declaration of Independence had been signed. Wister had an additional concern: He was a Quaker, a member of the Religious Society of Friends. As a Quaker, he opposed violence and refused to participate in the war. Quakers were often suspected of being loyal to King George III and, in fact, many Quakers were Loyalists. Wister, however, was sympathetic to the American cause. All things considered, he felt it was unwise to remain in Philadelphia. He and his family fled to a farm in North Wales, about 15 miles from the city.

The farm was owned by Hannah Foulke, who was connected to the Wisters by marriage. She and her three adult children welcomed Daniel and his wife, Lowry, as well as their children, Sarah (Sally), age 15; Elizabeth, 13; Hannah, 10; Susannah, 4; and John, 18 months. There was room for all in the large, two-story stone house.

Sally was kept informed about events "back home" by her friend Deborah Norris. In a letter dated January 27, 1777, Deborah wrote: "Our Philadelphia is not as it used to be. You can scarce walk a square without seeing the shocking sight of a Cart with five or Six Coffins in it. Oh! it is too dreadful a scene to Attempt to describe. . . . But I will drop this mournful subject, though my mind is full of it."

The Wisters and Foulkes were spared such sights in North Wales, but the war was never far away. Rumors that the English were about to take possession of Philadelphia disturbed Sally. In her journal she wrote: "The uncertainty of our position engrosses me quite. Perhaps to be in the midst of war, and ruin, and the clang of arms. But we must hope the best."

Sally addressed her journal entries to Deborah Norris. In the first entry, she explained that she had "not the least shadow of an opportunity to send a letter." Instead, she hoped Deborah would enjoy reading the entire journal at some future date. Entries were dated, and Sally followed the Quaker custom of identifying the days of the week as First Day, Second Day, and so forth.

On September 23, 1777, Philadelphia fell to the British. On September 24 the Wisters and Foulkes received a scare. Sally wrote: "About seven o'clock we heard a great noise. To the door we all went. A large number of waggons, with about three hundred of the Philadelphia Militia. They begged for drink, and several push'd into the house. One of those that entered was a little tipsy, and had a mind to be saucy."

Sally was "mightily scar'd" and "all in a shake with fear." Soon, however, she realized that most of the soldiers were behaving in a gentlemanly fashion. "My fears were in some measure dispell'd," she wrote, "tho' my teeth rattled, and my hand shook like an aspen leaf."

The residents of the Foulke farm were no doubt cheered by the resounding American victory at Saratoga, New York, in October. For Sally, however, life at the Foulke farm generally consisted of long, boring days on which nothing happened, interrupted by occasional moments of terrible fright. Once she and the others were told by a neighbor that Hessians—German troops employed by the British—had turned into the lane leading to the Foulke house.

"Oh! What shall we do?" Sally exclaimed.

"What will become of us?" cried twenty-one-year-old Lydia Foulke, whom Sally later described as "delicate" and "chicken-hearted."

The girls soon discovered that the warning was a false alarm.

On another occasion, Sally was standing in the kitchen when she heard someone scream, "Sally, Sally, here are the light horse!"

"Fear tack'd wings to my feet," Sally reported. "At the porch I stopt, and it really was the light horse."

To Sally's relief, the men of the light horse—lightly armed mounted troops—proved to be Americans and "perfectly civil."

Finally, on October 19, the situation took a pleasant turn for Sally when Mrs. Foulke agreed to provide quarters for American brigadier-general William Smallwood and his staff. In her journal Sally described their arrival: "In the evening his Generalship came with six attendants, which compos'd his family, a large guard of soldiers, a number of horses and baggage-waggons. The yard and house were in confusion, and glitter'd with military equipment. . . . How new is our situation! I feel in good spirits, though surrounded by an Army, the house full of officers, the yard alive with soldiers—very peaceable sort of men, tho'. They eat like other folks, talk like them, and behave themselves with elegance; so I will not be afraid of them, that I won't.

"Adieu," she wrote in closing. "I am going to my chamber to dream, I suppose, of bayonets and swords, sashes, guns, and epaulets."

In the next day's entry, Sally gave brief descriptions of the soldiers. The general, she stated, was "tall, portly, well made: a truly martial air." Colonel George Lyne was "monstrous tall & brown . . . almost worn to a skeleton, but very lively and talkative." Finally, saving the best for last, she confided to Deborah that one man in particular had caught her eye. At first Sally described him as "cross and reserv'd," then wondered if his silence might indicate that he was "not clever." Eventually, she realized he was simply shy.

"Well, here comes the glory, the Major, so bashful, so famous," she wrote. "He is about nineteen, nephew to the Gen'l."

"The Major" was William Truman Stoddert of Maryland. Although Stoddert was a soldier—a constant reminder that the country was at war—he was also an appealing young man. Sally set out to dazzle him, convinced that she would soon drive away his bashfulness. In her journal entry for October 20, she made a point of telling Deborah Norris: "[The officers] din'd with us. I was dressed in my chintz, and look'd smarter than night before."

Unlike many Quakers, Sally's family was wealthy. Instead of the extremely plain dresses worn by most Quaker women, she wore colorful, fashionable clothes. In her journal she described several of her favorite outfits, including "a new purple and white striped Persian, white petticoat, muslin apron, gauze cap, and handkerchief."

In addition to being well dressed, Sally was better educated than many girls of her day. It is believed that she attended a school run by Quaker Anthony Benezet. Deborah Norris was one of Benezet's students, and Sally stated that her friendship with Deborah began "at school." Under Benezet's direction, Sally would have studied not only reading, writing, and arithmetic, but also literature and the classics.

Tall with full, clear features, auburn hair, and a pleasing figure, Sally was certainly capable of making a favorable impression on

Major Stoddert, although she knew it might take time. On October 21 she wrote in her journal: "The Gen'l still here; the Major still bashful."

The ice finally broke one evening a few days later, while Sally sat at a table entertaining her baby brother, John. Stoddert pulled up a chair and began to play with the child.

"Prepare to hear amazing things," Sally wrote later. "One word brought on another, and we chatted the greatest part of the evening."

From then on, the Major was much more sociable. Sally was not surprised. "A stoic cou'd not resist such affable damsels as we are," she told Deborah Norris, referring to herself and Lydia Foulke.

Later, however, she confessed that Lydia seemed to attract more admirers. One was "a parson belonging to the Army . . . near seven foot high, thin and meagre, not a single personal charm, and very few mental ones." Another guest at the farm—appropriately named "Colonel Guest"—also had his eye on Lydia. According to Sally, he was "very pretty; a charming person."

"When will Sally's admirers appear?" she wrote then. "Why, Sally has not charms sufficient to pierce the heart of a soldier. But still I won't despair. Who knows what mischief I yet may do?"

In the meantime, British and American forces were up to their own kind of mischief. Determined to open up a supply route for troops stationed in Philadelphia, the British captured Fort Mercer and Fort Mifflin, located on the Delaware River. Patriot general George Washington, who had fallen into disfavor with a number of military leaders and politicians, was nearly ousted from his position as commander in chief.

At the Foulke farm, Sally bid farewell to General Smallwood and his officers and wondered if she would ever see Major Stoddert again. After a period of relative calm, she was again compelled to use exclamation points in her journal. On December 5 she wrote: "Oh, gracious! Debby, I am all alive with fear. The English have come out to attack (as we imagine) our army. They are on Chestnut Hill. . . . What will become of us, only six miles distant? I fear we shall be in the midst of it. Heaven defend us from so dreadful a sight."

As Sally sat in the parlor worrying about the impending battle, the door burst open. Major Stoddert stood before her. "The poor fellow," she wrote in her journal. "[He] had caught cold, which brought on a fever. He cou'd scarcely walk."

After Stoddert had been helped to a room, Sally went to see him. "Instead of the lively, alert, blooming Stodard, who was on his feet the instant we enter'd," she wrote to Deborah, "he look'd pale, thin, and dejected, too weak to rise."

In spite of his infirmity, Stoddert bowed and said, "How are you, Miss Sally?"

The next morning Stoddert was "rather more like himself," according to Sally. When Sally commented that his illness had probably saved him from injury in battle, he disagreed, saying that he would soon be with his comrades again, ready to fight.

"That was heroic," Sally noted.

With her favorite major in residence again, she took extra care with her appearance, putting on a "silk and cotton gown" for teatime. Sitting by herself later that afternoon, she began to worry again about the possibility of a battle taking place nearby.

"I got so low spirited that I cou'd hardly speak," she wrote in her journal. "And yet I did not feel half so frighten'd as I expected to be. 'Tis amazing how we get reconciled to such things. Six months ago the bare idea of being within ten, aye twenty miles, of a battle, wou'd almost have distracted me. And now . . . we can be cheerful and converse calmly of it."

In this particular instance she need not have worried. British general William Howe decided not to attack Washington's troops after all. Instead, Howe returned to Philadelphia and settled in for the winter.

Major Stoddert returned to his unit but was back at the Foulke farm by mid-December. During a conversation with Sally, he asked what she would do if the British were to come to the farm. Sally exclaimed that she would "be frightened just to death." Stoddert laughed and said she should "escape their rage" by getting behind the wooden representation of a British grenadier that was kept upstairs.

"We had brought some weeks ago a British grenadier from Uncle Miles's on purpose to divert us," Sally explained in her journal. "It is remarkably well executed, six foot high, and makes a martial appearance."

Stoddert confided to Sally that he would like to use the replica to frighten one of the other soldiers, Robert Tilly. Sally described Tilly as "a wild, noisy mortal . . . above the common size . . . a very great laugher." He kept her in "perpetual good humour" but also struck her as immature and foolish. Stoddert's proposition appealed to Sally, and she agreed to have the grenadier placed at the door that opened into the road.

That evening, as the men were sitting around "chatting on public affairs," a servant appeared and said, "There's somebody at the door that wishes to see you."

"All of us?" Tilly asked.

"Yes, sir," the servant replied.

Everyone besides Tilly was in on the joke and had trouble keeping straight faces as the group walked into the entryway. The wooden grenadier stood in the doorway. A voice thundered: "Is there any rebel officers here?"

Sally described what happened next: "Not waiting for a second word, [Tilly] darted like lightning out at the front door, through the yard, bolted o'er the fence. Swamps, fences, thorn-hedges, and plough'd fields no way impeded his retreat.

"Figure to thyself this Tilly," she wrote to Deborah. "Of a snowy even, no hat, shoes down at heel, hair unty'd, flying across meadows, creeks and mud-holes. Flying from what? Why, a bit of painted wood."

Stoddert staggered into the parlor, convulsed with laughter, and sank into an armchair.

"Go call Tilly back," Sally said, breathless with giggles. "He will lose himself—indeed he will."

Stoddert went to the door and called Tilly's name but received no answer. When Tilly did return, Sally admitted she felt sorry for him, "his fine hair hanging dishevell'd down his shoulders, all splashed with mud."

"You may all go to the D——l!" Tilly exclaimed, shocking Sally, who had "never heard him utter an indecent expression before."

At last, she reported, "his good nature gain'd a compleat ascendance over his anger, and he join'd heartily in the laugh. I will do him the justice to say that he bore it charmingly." She commented that whenever the subject came up again, "Our Tillian Hero gave a mighty droll account of his retreat, as they call it."

After such merriment, Sally hated to see the officers go away again. On December 20 she wrote in her journal: "General Washington's army have gone into winter quarters at Valley Forge. We shall not see many of the military now. We shall be very intimate with solitude. I am afraid stupidity will be a frequent guest."

During the ensuing weeks, Sally referred to the Foulke farm as a "nunnery." In early February she wrote: "Nothing happen'd all January that was uncommon." She made no entries between March 1 and May 11, 1778. On that day, she entered an explanation in the journal: "The scarcity of paper, which is very great in this part of the country, and the three last months producing hardly anything material, has prevented me from keeping a regular account of things; but to-day the scene begins to brighten, and I will continue my nonsense."

A fresh crop of soldiers had arrived. Sally filled the pages of her journal with descriptions of the men and related conversations she had with them. On the evening of June 3, a horseman arrived with the message: "Let the troop lie on their arms, and be ready to march at a moment's warning."

Frightened, Sally asked one of the men what was happening. He said the British were probably in motion.

"What will thee do if they come here?" Sally asked.

The answers was terse: "Defend the house as long as I can, ma'am."

Not long after that, a servant girl came running in, declaring that the lane was "filled with light horse." Sally looked out and saw that the girl was right. The group passed by, followed by "another party, much larger than the other, in dark clothes."

"These," she wrote in her journal, "we all thought were British. They halted. All as still as death."

The officer rode up to the door. As soon as he spoke, Sally recognized his voice as William Stoddert's. Two soldiers had deserted, he explained, and the regiment was moving to new quarters. After visiting for about fifteen minutes, he and the others departed.

"The moon at intervals broke thro' the heavy black clouds," Sally wrote. "No noise was perceiv'd, save that which the horses made as they trotted o'er the wooden bridge across the race. Echo a while gave us back the sound. At last nothing was left but the remembrance of them."

Sally made her last journal entry on June 20, 1778. Two days earlier, American troops had regained control of Philadelphia, and she looked forward to going home.

"[I] shall now conclude this journal," she wrote. "With humbly hoping that the Great Disposer of events, who had graciously vouchsaf'd to protect us to this day through many dangers, will still be pleas'd to continue his protection."

Although the journal was officially "closed," Sally jotted additional comments in the back from time to time. In July 1778 she wrote: "It has at length pleased the Almighty to restore us to our friends and native city. May I be grateful for this & every other blessing."

She added that she found "the rattling of carriages over the streets" to be "harsh music, tho' preferable to croaking frogs and screeching owls."

If Sally ever saw Major Stoddert again, there is no record of it. Even if she had, a serious relationship between the two would have been improbable. As a Quaker, Sally considered war to be un-Christian. Stoddert was a soldier. Not only that, Sally was forbidden to marry outside her faith, and Stoddert was a member of the Church of England.

Apparently Sally was kept informed—at least for a time—of the whereabouts and activities of her soldier friends. On January 4, 1780, she jotted in her journal: "The worthy Stodard is much indispos'd at his home in [Maryland]."

Sally might have been interested to learn that Stoddert married a woman with her name. In his will, probated August 17, 1793, he left his plantation and all his land to his wife, Sally.

Although Sally Wister clearly enjoyed socializing with the soldiers who came to the Foulke farm, she never married. She continued to write lively letters to family and friends, often in verse. Her poetry appeared in the Philadelphia *Portfolio*.

Sally's later years were occupied with religious matters. When she died in April 1804, the Wisters' family physician described her as a "shining example of prudence, virtue, piety, and eminent acquirements."

ALMOST BEYOND ENDURANCE

Christopher Hawkins

1764–1837

A cool breeze stirred fitfully in the thick, hazy air. Thunder rumbled. The signs were unmistakable that morning in the fall of 1777.

"We are soon to have a storm," said the captain of the *Eagle,* an American schooner headed home from British waters.

Most of the men on board already knew a storm was brewing. Not only that, they knew what to do about it. They were experienced "tars," so called because they used tar to waterproof their pants. As the breeze picked up and the sky darkened, they set about adjusting the sails. They lashed down the hatches and nailed tarpaulin over them. Every sailor did his part to secure the vessel.

The wind whipped itself into a gale. Lightning flashed. Swells rose to alarming heights, towered over the schooner, then swooped down across the deck.

Christopher Hawkins grabbed the rail as the *Eagle* heaved and lurched under his feet. Another salty wave smacked his face. The thirteen-year-old Rhode Island boy had spent the past five months getting his sea legs. Now he wondered whether those legs would continue to hold him upright. Even the more experienced sailors were sliding across the slick deck.

The storm blasted the *Eagle* throughout the evening and into the next day. The second night, the crew had to throw six of the heaviest cannons overboard to lighten the vessel. There was nothing to eat or drink on deck except bad water. As evening drew near again, some of the crew asked Capt. Mawry Potter if there was any food down below. He told them Christopher, the cabin boy, would know best.

Crew members opened the hatch and helped Christopher down into the companionway—a stairway leading to the deck below. He gathered as much food and drink as he could find, and the sailors hauled him up again.

"This was a very small meal for each of the crew when divided," Christopher wrote years later in his memoirs. "And nothing else could be obtained through the dismal and painful night ensuing—the gale was hard so that ev'ry one was either lashed to some part of the vessel, or clung to some of her rigging—no one slept."

On the morning of the third day, the wind seemed a bit calmer. Although swells continued to rise and roll, water did not break over the deck as often as it had before. Tired and hungry, the crew decided to seek food again in the vessel's hold.

"My share was a hard biscuit and small piece of raw pork," Christopher wrote. "This to me . . . was a delicious meal." As he ate, he thought about his journey so far, remembering how disoriented he had been his first few days on board. "I knew nothing of a seafaring life," he wrote. "For after the vessel had sailed from the sight of land, she seemed to me as steering in the same direction as when she left the Harbour."

Before too long Christopher got used to the shriek of the boatswain's whistle. He soon knew the words to the rhythmic chanties the men sang while they pulled on the rigging. He knew what the captain meant when he shouted "Avast!" or "Ready about!" through his trumpet. As cabin boy, Christopher's duties included keeping an eye on the sand glass. Every half hour, someone had to turn the sand glass over and ring the ship's bells to let everyone know the time.

Although Christopher found sea life interesting, the voyage had been something of a disappointment to him. The purpose of the trip was to pursue enemy ships, seize their cargo, and capture their crews. The crew of the *Eagle* had sailed all the way to England without encountering another ship.

On the way back to America, their luck finally changed. They came upon a vessel carrying French papers. However, the crew of the *Eagle* was certain it was a British vessel, not French. To their displeasure, Captain Potter refused to attack.

A couple of days later, a copper-bottomed British brig loomed into view. Its commander ignored Potter's order to come alongside, and the *Eagle* fired. "At this time my situation did not appear so pleasant to me," Christopher recalled in his memoirs. "The idea of broadsides, blood, death, etc., rather disturbed my mind, for the time being."

He need not have worried. Seeming to give in, the British commander asked Captain Potter to wait until morning to take possession of the brig, and Potter agreed. By daylight the British vessel was gone, having slipped away in the foggy darkness. Once again the *Eagle* had failed to take a prize. Then, shortly after that, a storm grabbed hold of the schooner and tossed it around like a toy.

Christopher sighed. He was serving on the *Eagle* by choice, but he had to admit he would not mind feeling the dependable streets of Providence, Rhode Island, beneath his feet again.

Born on June 8, 1764, Christopher was the blue-eyed and black-haired son of Hezabiah and Abigail Patt Hawkins, both natives of Rhode Island. He was one of thirteen children.

The American Revolution came early to Christopher's hometown of Providence. He was barely eight years old when a group of Providence men set fire to the British schooner *Gaspee* in Narragansett Bay. King George III had sent the *Gaspee* to put a stop to the brisk smuggling trade harbored by Rhode Island's coves and inlets. Smugglers evaded the duties and taxes levied by the Crown, depriving the Mother Country of precious income.

In 1775, when Christopher was eleven years old, he was "bound out" to Aaron Mason, a tanner. This arrangement allowed the boy to learn a trade as Mason's apprentice, while Mason provided him with room and board. By that time Providence was home to more than 4,500 people. Its many thriving businesses included distilleries, candle works, tanneries, sugar houses, chocolate houses, gristmills, a slaughter house, a potash works, and a paper mill.

As a tanner's apprentice, Christopher learned how to immerse animal hides in a mixture of water and tannin, a chemical found in tree leaves and bark. The material was then dyed and rubbed with waxes or grease if desired, and the end result was leather. Tanning was a smelly process; workers risked getting anthrax (sometimes called hoof-and-mouth disease) and tetanus, or lockjaw.

Fortunately, Christopher did not come down with anthrax or lockjaw. He did, however, catch the "patriotism bug." It was not hard to do in Providence, where devotion to the rebel cause ran high. On May 4, 1776, two months before the Continental Congress declared independence, Rhode Island voted to dissolve its allegiance to King George III.

At the beginning of the Revolution, America had no navy. What America did have, especially in Rhode Island, were able-bodied, experienced "tars." These men set out on privateers, privately owned ships authorized by Congress. The *Eagle* was such a ship.

"In the month of May 1777," Christopher wrote in his memoirs, "I left Mr. Aaron Mason . . . went to New Bedford, Massachusetts, and entered on board a privateer Schooner, mounting twelve small carriage guns, by the name of the *Eagle*, Mowry Potter, Master."

For Christopher, who would be thirteen years old in about a month, the adventures promised by privateering were highly preferable to learning the tanning business. He may have been inspired by newspaper ads like the following, which appeared in the *Boston Gazette:*

> The grand Privateer Ship DEANE . . . will hail on a Cruise against the Enemies of the United States of America . . . This therefore is to invite all those Jolly Fellows, who love their Country, and want to make their Fortunes at one Stroke, to repair immediately to the Rendezvous at the Head of His Excellency Governor Hancock's Wharf, where they will be received with a hearty Welcome by a Number of Brave Fellows there assembled . . .

Now, as Christopher munched his hard tack, or sea biscuit as it was sometimes called, he wondered if he would receive any payment at all, let alone a "Fortune."

"I was in a rather melancholy mood," he wrote later, "and cast my eyes about hoping to discover land—in this endeavor . . . I discovered something in appearance resembling a very small bush without leaves."

What Christopher saw was a sail. The crew grew excited, thinking it must be the British brig that had escaped their clutches earlier. Soon the *Eagle* was in pursuit. But as they drew closer, the other boat turned and headed toward the *Eagle*.

"It was our ill fate to learn that she was an English sloop of war—the *Sphynx* of twenty guns," Christopher recalled. "Our course immediately shifted from a *chase* to a *run away*."

Unfortunately, the *Eagle* could not run fast enough or far enough to escape the British vessel. Christopher was taken aboard the captain's barge, which carried him from the *Eagle* to the *Sphynx*.

"Many ropes were thrown to us from on board," he later wrote. "I fast'ned the end of one around my breast, and called to those on deck to 'haul away'—some one cried out on the quarter deck, 'Put it round your d——d neck you d——d yankee, and we'll soon haul you up!'"

A British officer intervened, and Christopher was hauled aboard. The pewter buttons on his clothing drew the attention of the enemy crew. The buttons bore the motto "Liberty and Property," which, in Christopher's words did not "suit their taste quite so well." One of his captors called for a knife to cut off the buttons, but again an officer interceded.

Christopher watched as the British sank the *Eagle*. Most of the crew was confined to the cable tier of the *Sphynx*, down in the bottom of the ship, but Christopher fared better. He and another boy, Paul, were "allowed to run about deck and between decks among the common sailors, who fed us with as much food as we wanted."

This "playtime" did not last. The British captain announced that the boys would be interrogated. The boatswain's mate stood nearby, flicking a whipping instrument called a cat-o-nine-tails, or "cat." First, the mate tied Paul to a gun. Christopher later recalled: "The sight of the cat and the process of tieing moved Paul's feelings so much that he bawled out with terror—he made a noise as loud as a mad bull."

Christopher was tied to another gun. The captain began to question Paul, but Christopher later reported that "the bawling of Paul prevented me from hearing much if any of their dialogue." When Christopher's turn came, he answered the captain's questions willingly. His account of the brig that snuck away in the night amused his captors greatly, much to Christopher's displeasure.

Finally, the *Sphynx* reached New York, which had been under British control for more than a year. Christopher and his fellow privateers were transferred to a prison ship. After about three weeks, Christopher was taken to the British frigate *Maidstone* to serve as a waiter. He and an English boy named Stephen were assigned to the same officer. Stephen was three or four years older than Christopher and tended to get drunk. Because Christopher was more reliable, Stephen was told to follow the thirteen-year-old's direction regarding cooking, cleaning the cabin, and so forth. Not surprisingly, the English boy resented the arrangement.

"On one occasion," Christopher later recalled, "my Stephen did not clean the knives and forks in a proper manner for which I called him to an account. . . . [He] stabbed me with a table fork. . . .The blood soon made its appearance running down my clothes freely."

Several British sailors witnessed the attack. Stephen was brutally punished, even though Christopher attempted to intervene on his behalf. "The witnessing of this punishment and the shrieks of the sufferer made me sick at the stomach," he wrote.

From the outset, Christopher looked for ways to escape. Unfortunately, he was only allowed on shore once during the *Maidstone*'s fifteen-month cruise. He was part of a group of boys who went ashore on a small island to gather twigs to make brooms.

One day the *Maidstone* captured a French vessel. Christopher's master was given command of the prize, and Christopher accompanied him. The men assigned to the captured ship could best be described as a "skeleton crew." According to Christopher they were "indifferent" and "composed mostly of invalids."

Some of them were also highly superstitious. Christopher found their fears amusing. He liked to tell about the time an old English sailor ran up to him and several others on the quarter-deck. Clearly alarmed, the old fellow declared that the vessel was haunted. He insisted he had heard a scratching sound and a voice saying "quit." Christopher investigated and heard the voice himself. It seemed to come from under an old tarpaulin.

"I removed the tarpaulin," he later wrote, "and a large cock Turkey appeared. I loudly observed that I had found the spirit."

Finally the captured vessel reached New York, and Christopher was allowed to go ashore whenever he wanted. One morning he was sent into town with clothing to be washed. An English boy named William Rock had to run a similar errand, and the two set out together. Christopher decided it was a good time to escape and told William his intention. To Christopher's surprise, the English boy wanted to go with him. Christopher tried to discourage him, but William insisted. The Rhode Islander soon found out that William had odd ideas about America. As the boys walked down a New York street, William said: "When you do get [to America] the wild beasts will tear you in pieces."

Christopher discovered that William thought New York was "a British port" and that America was filled with wild beasts and savages. Laughing, the Rhode Islander assured him that "the greater portion of New England was wholly exempted from the incursions of wild beasts and savages."

Christopher, now age fourteen, led the way. As he and William prepared to take the ferry to Brooklyn, a third escapee joined them. He was John Sawyer, an American boy from Long Island. John had been a prisoner on the *Maidstone*, where he served as the captain's clerk. Soon the three boys were headed for Sag Harbor, where John's uncle lived.

Although they were stopped several times by suspicious British soldiers, they had made up a story about who they were and where they were going. They were allowed to continue. In Sag Harbor, John's uncle arranged for William and Christopher to travel across the sound. He cautioned them, Christopher recalled, saying, "Boys there are British officers walking our streets in disguise."

Christopher and William spent the night at Saybrook Point. The next morning, when Christopher looked for William, he discovered that the English boy had joined the British army. Mortified, Christopher tried to get his friend released, but he did not succeed.

When Christopher finally returned home to Providence in November 1778, his family was overjoyed to see him. He worked on a farm for two or three years, but missed life on the high seas. Following an argument with some of his fellow laborers, he signed up for duty on a brig.

At age sixteen, Christopher became a sailor once again. This time he was only onboard a few days when the brig was captured. Along with the rest of the crew, Christopher was placed down in the cable tier of the British frigate. The situation was, in his words, "uncomfortable almost beyond endurance."

"We were so crowded," he wrote later, "that we could not either sit or lie down."

In spite of their discomfort, the Americans entertained the British with patriotic songs. "The singing was excellent and its volume was extensive," Christopher wrote, "and yet extremely harsh to the taste of the captors. The guard frequently threatened to fire upon us if the singing was not dispensed with . . . They only brought forth higher notes and vociferous defiance from the crew."

The American captives were taken to New York, where they were imprisoned on the *Jersey*, a worn-down British vessel that had begun the Revolution as a hospital ship. Converted to a prison ship in the winter of 1779–1780, the *Jersey* became infamous as a floating trash heap filled with disease, despair, and death.

Here there was no singing. Many prisoners were sick with dysentery. Most were covered with vermin such as lice and fleas. Christopher and his crewmate William Waterman made a quick decision. "We had not been on board the 'Old Jersey' more than one hour before we began to plot our escape," Christopher recalled.

The two managed to create an escape route by cutting through the bars on one of the gun ports. They planned to lower themselves through the opening with a rope, then swim 2½ miles in chilly October waters. All this would have to be done without drawing the attention of the guards.

The odds were long, but Christopher and William were determined. On the night of their third day of captivity, they packed their clothing in knapsacks, which they fastened to their backs. William left the ship first. Christopher waited about a minute, then slipped through the hole. He knew if any of the soldiers guarding the *Jersey* heard him, he would face cruel punishment or even death.

"The weather was mild and hazy," Christopher wrote in his memoirs, "and the night extremely dark. . . . I could take my course very well from the light reflected from the stern lanthrons of the [ships], and also from the responses of the sentinels on shore, in the words 'all's well.' These responses were repeated ev'ry half hour."

Christopher had been swimming nearly two hours when his knapsack broke loose from his back. He tried to hold onto the bag with one arm and swim with the other. That did not work, so he pulled the edge of his vest out of the knapsack and took it between his teeth. He later remarked that he felt like a fox carrying a stolen goose off to its den.

"My load cramped my neck," he wrote, "and I had now become chilled from the coolness of the water." Numb with cold, he again tried to swim with the bag under one arm. Finally, he gave up and let the knapsack go. By the time he reached the shore, he was so exhausted he could only fall down and sleep. When he woke up he had another problem to face. "I was completely naked except a small hat on my head," he recalled.

Making his way across the countryside in such a vulnerable state was a challenge. While hiding in a barn, he tried to milk a cow to satisfy his craving for food. The cows were uncooperative. "They were so afraid of my naked situation that I was not suffered to get near them," he wrote. "If I attempted it, they would run and snuff like deers."

Christopher traveled through fields and thickets, surviving on frostbitten watermelon and corn. Chilly rain fell in torrents and he found shelter where he could. Finally, he encountered two young men who took pity on him and gave him clothing and food. At long last he reached Sag Harbor and stayed with John Sawyer's uncle for a time. From there he eventually made his way to Providence, where he took up farming again. His seafaring days were over. Although Christopher never saw William Waterman again, he later heard he had safely reached home.

At age twenty, Christopher Hawkins married Dorcas Whipple of Smithfield, Rhode Island. The couple eventually became the first permanent settlers of Newport, New York. They had seven children: Susannah, Amy, Catharine, Christopher, Nancy, Experience, and Abigail.

As an adult Christopher was described as industrious, kind-hearted, and charitable, with a somewhat sarcastic sense of humor. He worked mostly as a farmer and occasionally as a carpenter.

Christopher Hawkins wrote his memoirs in 1834 at age seventy, three years before his death. In the introduction to his memoirs, he stated, "My principal design is to amuse and inform my friends and descendents with the sufferings of my youth."

In doing so, he provided generations to come with a glimpse into the earliest days of a brand-new nation.

BIBLIOGRAPHY

General References

Axelrod, Alan, Ph.D. *The Complete Idiot's Guide to the American Revolution*. Indianapolis, Ind.: Alpha Books, 2000.

The Blackwell Encyclopedia of the American Revolution, edited by Jack P. Greene and J. R. Pole. Malden, Mass.: Blackwell Publishers Inc., 1991.

Chapelle, Howard I. *The History of American Sailing Ships*. New York: W. W. Norton & Company, Inc., 1935.

Coggins, Jack. *Ships and Seamen of the American Revolution*. Harrisburg, Pa.: The Stackpole Company, 1969.

Earle, Alice Morse. *Child Life in Colonial Days*. New York: The Macmillan Company, 1899.

Haven, Kendall. *Voices of the American Revolution*. Englewood, Colo.: Libraries Unlimited, Inc., 2000.

Lossing, Benson J. *The Pictorial Field-Book of the Revolution*, vol. 1. New York: Harper & Brothers, Publishers, 1859.

Middlekauff, Robert. *The Glorious Cause: The American Revolution, 1763–1789*. New York and Oxford: Oxford University Press, 1982.

Raphael, Ray. *A People's History of the American Revolution*. New York: The New Press, 2001.

Taylor, Dale. *The Writer's Guide to Everyday Life in Colonial America*. Cincinnati, Ohio: Writer's Digest Books, 1997.

Zall, P. M. *Becoming American: Young People in the American Revolution*. Hamden, Conn.: Linnet Books, 1993.

John Greenwood

Greenwood, John. *A Young Patriot in the American Revolution, 1775–1783*. Tyrone, Pa.: Westvaco, 1981.

Background note on John Greenwood Journal at William L. Clements Library, The University of Michigan Web site: www.clements.umich.edu/Webguides/G/Greenwood.html. Accessed May 2003.

"Learning About George Washington," Webquest GW Web site: gwpapers.virginia.edu/lesson/wqteacher.html. Accessed May 2003.

"Songs and Ballads of the American Revolution," with notes and illustrations by Frank Moore. New York: D. Appleton & Company, 1855.

Andrew Sherburne

Coggins, Jack. *Ships and Seamen of the American Revolution*. Harrisburg, Pa.: Stackpole Books, 1969.

Lemisch, Jesse. "A Short Life of Andrew Sherburne, a Pensioner of the Navy of the Revolution," *The Colonel's Hat, A History of the Township of Augusta*, Stella Cieslak et al., eds. Mohawk Valley, N.Y.: Mohawk Valley Printing Co., 1977.

Sherburne, Andrew. *The Memoirs of Andrew Sherburne: Patriot and Privateer of the American Revolution*, edited by Karen Zeinert. Hamden, Conn.: Linnet Books, 1993.

Turner, Lynn Warren. *The Ninth State: New Hampshire's Formative Years*. Chapel Hill: The University of North Carolina Press, 1983.

"Vessels of the Continental Navy," Department of the Navy—Naval Historical Center Web site: www.history.navy.mil/wars/revwar/contships.htm. Accessed May 2003.

Mary Hunt Palmer

Adams, Charles Francis. *Three Episodes of Massachusetts History, Vol. II*. Boston: Houghton, Mifflin and Company, 1903.

Barber, John Warner. *Historical Collections*. Worcester, Mass.: Dorr, Howland & Co., 1840.

Carson, Ada Lou, and Herbert L. Carson. *Royall Tyler*. Boston: Twayne Publishers, 1979.

Nelson-Burns, Lesley, "Popular Songs in American History" Web site: www.contemplator.com/america/freeamer.html. Accessed May 2003.

Tanselle, G. Thomas. *Royall Tyler*. Cambridge, Mass.: Harvard University Press, 1967.

Tyler, Mary Palmer. *Grandmother Tyler's Book*. New York: G. P. Putnam's Sons, 1925.

Watts, Isaac. Poem posted on Christian Classics Ethereal Library at Calvin College Web site, www.ccel.org/.

James Durham

Cox, Clinton. *African American Healers*. New York: John Wiley, 2000.

Drinker, Elizabeth. *The Diary of Elizabeth Drinker, Vol. I*. Boston: Northeastern University Press, 1991.

Kopperman, Paul E. "Medical Services in the British Army, 1742–1783." *Journal of the History of Medicine* (October 1979): 428–55.

Marshall, Christopher. *Extracts from the Diary of Christopher Marshall, 1774–1781*, edited by William Duane. New York: The New York Times & Arno Press, 1969.

Middleton, W. S. "The John Kearsleys." *Annals of Medical History*, vol. 3 (1921): 392–402.

Moore, Frank. "Diary of the American Revolution, Vol. I." New York: Charles Scribner; London: Sampson Low, Son & Company, 1860. Accessed online at 3mpub.com/carper/.

Ousterhout, Anne M. "Controlling the Opposition in Pennsylvania During the American Revolution." *The Pennsylvania Magazine of History and Biography* CV, no. 1 (January 1981): 3–11.

Plummer, Betty L. "Letters of James Durham to Benjamin Rush." *Journal of Negro History* 65, no. 3 (summer 1980): 261–69.

Rush, Benjamin. *Letters of Benjamin Rush*, edited by L. H. Butterfield. Princeton, N.J.: Princeton University Press, 1951.

Wynes, Charles E. "Dr. James Durham, Mysterious Eighteenth-Century Black Physician: Man or Myth?" *The Pennsylvania Magazine of History and Biography* (July 1979): 325–33.

Deborah Samson

"An Address Delivered in 1802 in Various Towns in Massachusetts, Rhode Island, and New York by Mrs. Deborah Sampson Gannett." Reprinted by the Sharon Historical Society, 1905.

De Pauw, Linda Grant. *Battle Cries and Lullabies: Women in War from Prehistory to the Present*. Norman, Okla.: University of Oklahoma Press, 2000.

"Diary of Deborah Sampson Gannett in 1802" (facsimile). Courtesy of Sharon Public Library, Sharon, Massachusetts.

Freeman, Lucy, and Alma Halbert Bond, Ph.D. *America's First Woman Warrior*. New York: Paragon House, 1992.

Hiltner, Judith, "'The Example of our Heroine': Deborah Sampson and the Legacy of Herman Mann's *The Female Review.*" *American Studies* 41, no. 1 (spring 2000).

Moody, Pauline. *Massachusetts' Deborah Sampson*. Privately published, 1975.

Vinton, John Adams, ed. *The Female Review: Life of Deborah Sampson, the Female Soldier in the War of the Revolution*. Boston: J. K. Wiggin & Wm. Parsons Lunt, 1866.

Vitzhum, Richard G. *Land and Sea: The Lyric Poetry of Philip Freneau*. Minneapolis: University of Minnesota Press, 1978.

Ebenezer Fox

E-mail correspondence with descendants of Ebenezer Fox, June 2003.

Fox, Ebenezer. *The Revolutionary Adventures of Ebenezer Fox of Roxbury Massachusetts*. Boston: Munroe & Frances, 1838.

Massachusetts Soldiers and Sailors of the Revolutionary War, compiled by Secretary of the Commonwealth. Boston: Wright & Potter Printing Co., 1899, vol. 5, p. 961.

Narratives of the American Revolution, edited by Hugh F. Rankin. Chicago: R. R. Donnelley & Sons Company, 1976.

James Potter Collins

Babits, Lawrence E. *Cowpens Battlefield, A Walking Guide*. Johnson City, Tenn.: Overmountain Press, 1993.

Brakebill, Clovis H. *American Revolutionary Soldiers Buried in Texas*. Wolfe City, Tex.: Texas Society, Sons of the American Revolution, 1998.

Buchanan, John. *The Road to Guilford Courthouse: The American Revolution in the Carolinas*. New York: John Wiley & Sons, 1997.

Collins, James Potter. A *Revolutionary Soldier* (revised and prepared by John M. Roberts). New York: Arno Press, 1979.

New York Journal, February 9, 1775, as quoted in *Diary of the American Revolution from Newspapers and Original Documents, Vol. 1*, by Frank Moore. New York: Charles Scribner, 1860.

Frances Slocum

Axtell, James. "The White Indians of Colonial America." *William and Mary Quarterly*, Third Series, volume 32, issue 1 (January 1975): 55–88.

Campbell, Thomas. "Gertrude of Wyoming," from *The Poetical Works of Thomas Campbell*. New York: Leavitt & Allen, 1865.

Dye, Kitty. *Maconaquah's Story: The Saga of Frances Slocum*, 2nd edition. Port Clinton, Ohio: LeClere Publishing Company, 2000.

Meginness, John F. *Biography of Frances Slocum, the Lost Sister of Wyoming*. New York: Arno Press, 1974 (originally published in 1891 by Heller Bros. Printing House of Williamsport, Pa.).

Weslager, C. A. *The Delaware Indians, A History*. New Brunswick, N.J.: Rutgers University Press, 1972.

Wilson, William E. "Frances Slocum: 'The Lost Sister.'" *American History Illustrated* 3, no. 8 (August 1968).

Winger, Otho. *The Lost Sister among the Miamis*. Elgin, Ill.: Elgin Press, 1938.

James Forten

Douty, Esther M. *Forten the Sailmaker: Pioneer Champion of Negro Rights*. Chicago: Rand McNally, 1968.

Gloucester, S. H. "A discourse delivered on the occasion of the death of Mr. James Forten, Sr." Philadelphia: I. Ashmead and Co., 1848.

Nash, Gary B. *Forging Freedom: The Formation of Philadelphia's Black Community, 1720–1840*. Cambridge, Mass.: Harvard University Press, 1988.

Purvis, Robert. "Remarks on the Life and Character of James Forten." Philadelphia: Merrihew and Thompson, 1842.

Quarles, Benjamin. *The Negro in the American Revolution*. Chapel Hill: The University of North Carolina Press, reprint edition, 1996.

Winch, Julie. *A Gentleman of Color: The Life of James Forten*. Oxford University Press, 2002.

Sally Wister

Booth, Sally Smith. *The Women of '76*. New York: Hastings House, 1973.

O'Hara, Megan, ed. *A Colonial Quaker Girl: The Diary of Sally Wister, 1777–1778*. Mankato, Minn.: Blue Earth Books, 2000.

Wister, Sally. *Sally Wister's Journal*, edited by Albert Cook Myers. Philadelphia: Ferris & Leach, 1969.

Christopher Hawkins

Chapelle, Howard I. *The History of American Sailing Ships*. New York: W. W. Norton & Company, 1935.

Conley, Patrick T. "Revolution's Impact on Rhode Island." *Rhode Island History* 34, no. 4 (November 1975): 121–28.

Hawkins, Christopher. *The Adventures of Christopher Hawkins*. New York: Privately printed, 1864.

Wilbur, C. Keith. *Picture Book of the Revolution's Privateers*. Harrisburg, Pa.: The Stackpole Company, 1973.

INDEX

ABOUT THE AUTHOR

Scotti McAuliff Cohn is a freelance writer and copy editor living and working in Bloomington, Illinois. She has written three other books for The Globe Pequot Press: *More than Petticoats: Remarkable North Carolina Women*; *It Happened in North Carolina*; and *Beyond Their Years: Stories of Sixteen Civil War Children*.